Justice is Blind—

AND HER DOG
JUST PEED
IN MY
CORNFLAKES

Justice is Blind—

AND HER DOG
JUST PEED
IN MY
CORNFLAKES

Gordon Kirkland

HARBOUR PUBLISHING

Second Printing, 2000

Harbour Publishing
P.O. Box 219
Madeira Park, BC V0N 2H0 Canada

Harbour Publishing acknowledges the financial support of the
Government of Canada through the Canada Council for the Arts
and the Book Publishing Industry Development Program
(BPIDP) and the Province of British Columbia through the
British Columbia Arts Council for its publishing activities.

Cover design and illustration by Warren Clark

Canadian Cataloguing in Publication Data

Kirkland, Gordon, 1953–
   Justice is blind—and her dog just peed in my cornflakes

   ISBN 1-55017-198-4

   1. Canadian wit and humor (English)* I. Title.
PN6178.C3K57 1999   C818'.5402   C99-910311-3

THE CANADA COUNCIL | LE CONSEIL DES ARTS
FOR THE ARTS | DU CANADA
SINCE 1957 | DEPUIS 1957

To Diane, Mike and Brad
without whom my life
would have a lot less laughter

Contents

I May Not Be Handy, but I've Got All My Fingers

Society Is a Box of Chocolates with Too Many Nuts

Acknowledgments

Alot of people deserve thanks for getting me to this point, in particular, Cate McGarrell for proofreading, Roger Shick for helping maintain whatever level of sanity I have, Norbert Cunningham for giving me my start and everyone at the Pacific Northwest Writers Association for helping me get this book off the ground. I also have to thank Wayne Turner who's always been there with a screwdriver when I needed it.

There is, however, one person I will never get the opportunity to thank, but who, in his own way, is responsible for my taking that final step toward being a writer.

The late American humorist Lewis Grizzard won't know how important he's been in my life unless he can get a copy of this book on whatever piece of heavenly real estate he now occupies. He died in 1994 at the much too young age of forty-seven as doctors tried to save his life with yet another in a long series of heart-valve replacements.

Grizzard often wrote about his health problems. He approached them in his own irreverent style, making the reader laugh and cry at the same time. His acceptance of his condition, his ability to laugh at it and his desire to let others share in that laughter saw me through the darkest days after my spine was broken. I was in a Vancouver hospital, thinking—make that believing—my life was finished and reading his final book, *I Took a Beating and Kept on Ticking,* when I received a call telling me he was gone.

I didn't know whether I was crying for him, or me.

I think of him often when I'm writing. I wish I could share these stories with him. I wish he could share some more of his with me. Thanks, Lewis. One of these days we'll share a heavenly chili *dawg* in some celestial version of Atlanta's Victory Drive-in.

I'm buyin'.

INTRODUCTION

I Always Wanted to Be a Writer, and Now I Are Won

These pages contain the best of nearly four years of my syndicated newspaper column, "At Large." It's a mixture of stories from my life, my family—both nuclear and extended—and the way I look at other people's lives when they are reported in the media.

My life has been filled with laughter. From my earliest memories on, it's the laughter that stands out, not the tears. Our family dinners bore no resemblance to those seen in the Cleaver household we watched on *Leave It to Beaver*. Looking back, I think my family was more like *Monty Python's Flying Circus* meets *Rowan & Martin's Laugh-In*.

My life in the nineties has been a roller-coaster ride. The decade started with the release of my first books, six dull and boring texts about international trade. That wasn't the kind of writer I had dreamed of becoming back in Pat

Cole's high school English class in London, Ontario, in 1972.

Thoughts of any kind of career were put on hold in August 1990 when I sustained a severe spinal injury in a golfing accident. No, I didn't play full-contact golf. While I was on my way to a course, my car was rear-ended by a man looking for a cassette tape on the floor of his car. It really screwed up my handicap.

The next two years were spent in various forms of therapy and frustration while the effects of the injury took full control of my life. Just after the second anniversary of the accident, in August 1992, when I started to make my first attempts at "walking" again, a severely hung-over driver rear-ended my car and eliminated what few gains I had made. I spent the next two months in the hospital trying to rebuild my life as well as my body.

Two years later, in May 1994, I started to believe that even-numbered years in the nineties were out to get me. I was rear-ended again, this time by a member of the Royal Canadian Mounted Police. It was the fastest I had ever seen the police on the scene of an accident. The officer told me it was the fastest *he* had ever arrived on the scene of an accident.

A few months after that third accident, and twenty-two years after I left Pat Cole's classroom, I made my debut as a columnist in the *Times and Transcript* of Moncton, New Brunswick. Finally, after seeing that first *Times and Transcript* byline, I could call myself a writer and believe it. Syndication began a year and a half later.

I hope my readers have had as much fun reading about my life and times as I have had writing—and living—them.

Married Bliss
Isn't Always
an Oxymoron

It's Always Okay to Laugh—
Unless It's at Me

Despite living with me all these years, my family doesn't seem to understand when something is funny and when it's not. I'm writing this so that they, and anyone similarly humor-challenged, might gain a bit of understanding about when it's appropriate to laugh and when it's not.

Basically it all comes down to who's involved in an event. For example, if something amusingly unpleasant, scary, disgusting or even mildly painful happens to someone in my family, it's funny, and therefore it's appropriate to laugh. However, if something completely and utterly unpleasant happens to me, the other members of the clan should realize that isn't funny at all and refrain from laughing—at least until I can't hear them.

An example of a humorous household incident occurred a few years ago. I entered a contest that required me to take twenty photographs in the order they appeared on a list. One of them called for an interesting scene that included an insect. At this point, I should say that my wife, Diane, is terrified of anything that remotely resembles a spider. If she turns the page in a magazine and sees a picture of one, the book will fly across the room.

Mike, my oldest grocery-sucking-appetite-on-legs, got a realistic plastic spider from one of those vending machines that gives a two-cent toy in return for fifty cents. I placed the toy spider inside a carefully drained egg, with a couple of legs appearing out of the cracked shell.

The egg was placed—and looked quite photogenic, I might add—on the egg shelf in the refrigerator. After I photographed the scene, I went on to take the other pictures on the list. In my haste, I forgot to remove the eggshell that held the spider.

As soon as I heard the scream, I remembered the egg. When I got to the kitchen, Diane was just regaining consciousness on the floor in front of the open refrigerator.

Obviously the scene of my semiconscious, arachniphobic wife, who had discovered the realistic spider emerging from an egg in the refrigerator, might well be considered funny. Laughing at it would be a completely natural reaction. Diane didn't understand that, though, and as a result of her underdeveloped sense of humor, became quite annoyed at my laughter.

On the other hand, an event that could never possibly be considered humorous occurred more recently. I opened the refrigerator and spotted a snack item that my sons had obviously overlooked. There, on a plate, wrapped in cellophane, was some leftover pâté.

I spread a generous helping on a cracker and quickly discovered why no one had eaten the rest of this culinary delight. It tasted terrible. I rewrapped it and returned it to the refrigerator because I knew there was one person in the household who could eat disgusting things like broccoli without gagging, so I assumed the pâté belonged to her.

When I mentioned my unappetizing experience to Diane, she gave me one of her deer-caught-in-the-headlights looks and said, "You didn't . . . ?"

She tried to tell me I had eaten cat food, but I pointed out that the cat food was clearly visible on another shelf.

"Dear," she said, already starting to laugh, "I put cat food on that plate and mixed in the cat's antiflea medicine to make it easier to give to her."

This wasn't funny at all, because it didn't happen to one of them. If it had, we could have all shared a good laugh. Unfortunately my humor-challenged spouse didn't understand the important difference in this situation.

Of course, she didn't want to keep her misplaced hilarity to herself, so she immediately shared my misfortune with my equally humor-deficient sons. They, too, laughed uproariously. Another round of laughter ensued when one of them questioned my intelligence for even thinking he might have left an uneaten snack in the refrigerator for me to find.

And did they let it drop? No way. Hours later, when I sat down at the dinner table, I discovered I had been served cat food.

"We know it's your favorite, Dad," said Brad, my younger grocery-sucking-appetite-on-legs.

Despite my misfortune, and the annoyance I felt at my family's lack of understanding about when—and when not to—laugh, I was still able to find an upside to this event. When flea season starts, the animals and I won't have anything to worry about.

I'm Sure Glad My Wife Didn't Give Birth on the Internet

Not so long ago a woman gave birth during a live broadcast on the Internet. It was a nice, private affair attended by her physicians, her family and ten thousand complete strangers who were "lucky" enough to log on to her Web page in time for the blessed event.

I guess I should have expected it. Various Web pages around the Internet have been showing scenes of real or imagined conception for years. I guess this is a logical progression. Having been in the room for the birth of one of my sons, I can assure anyone who has not had the pleasure that it really wasn't much of a pleasure.

Oh, I know, I know. I'm going to get all kinds of letters from people telling me what a beautiful thing the birth experience is.

Beautiful?

Exciting maybe. Perhaps awe-inspiring. I'll even go as far as euphoric. But beautiful? I don't think so. The whole thing looked as if someone were trying to squeeze a wet cat through a hole in a balloon.

Of course, I realize everyone's experience is unique. We always hear about those women who wake up on their due date, realize they are in labor, decide to rewallpaper the nursery, bake a couple of loaves of bread, drive themselves to the hospital and painlessly give birth to a set of twins an hour later. We also hear about tooth fairies, flying reindeer and effective members of the Canadian, or American, Senate.

Both my sons wanted to stay in the warm comfort of their private wombs for as long as possible. The oldest resisted the forces of Diane's organized labor for a full forty-three hours. The second found a way to prevent labor even starting until a full three weeks after he was scheduled to make his appearance. Thirty-eight hours of labor later, he came into the world by Cesarean section. He still has no concept of time. It does, however, explain the boys' fondness for pizza. One was delivered and the other was take-out.

Fathers don't get much credit for what they go through dealing with the delivery of a child. We're about as important as the movie extra in the third row of the crowd scene in *Godzilla*. We're there, we're needed to make the scene complete and there is a screaming monster threatening to do bodily harm if she can get her hands on us, but you're not going to hear a word in the reviews about our importance to the production.

Women talk about the agony they had to endure to give life to their offspring. No one cares about the agony of the father. I tried holding my wife's hand in the delivery room. When a contraction hit, I thought my hand had been run over by a bus. Professional wrestlers could never hope to develop a grip like that. When I finally managed to free my hand, another contraction kicked in, and she grabbed my arm. I still have an outline of her fingernails clearly visible in my upper arm. Did any of the medical staff offer me an epidural? Of course not. I'm just the father.

I firmly believe that letting fathers into the delivery room is the single greatest reason the postwar baby boom ended. We went through the first twenty years after the Second World War with babies popping out all over. In the late sixties and early seventies, when fathers started staying with their wives instead of going outside where it was safe, the birth rate dropped faster than you could say, "You want me to do *what* to the umbilical cord?"

If the governments of Third World countries want to slow their population growth, they should insist that fathers go into the labor rooms. It will be more effective than all the birth-control programs put together.

I know it worked for me.

When we arrived at the hospital prior to the birth of our youngest son, I stayed behind filling out forms while Diane was taken to the maternity ward. I was understandably concerned for her well-being, and secretly even more concerned for my own. After all, it had only been two and a half years since our first child, and the memories of the pain I went through that time were still fresh. I was also trying to remember those breathing exercises we learned in prenatal class the first time around. I didn't want anyone hyperventilating in the delivery room the way I did the first time. Sensing my apprehension, the nurse tried to get me talking.

"Is this your first?" she asked.

"No," I replied. "This is definitely my last."

A Cut Below the Belt

"You may experience some minor discomfort."

If someone says that to you before you enter a dressing room full of sweaty teenage hockey players, it will be pretty much to the point. If doctors say it, they are lying.

I'm convinced the above warning is taught in medical school to be used: (a) when the doctor has no idea what it feels like to have done what he is suggesting; or (b) when he thinks you might be scared off if he told you the truth and he would lose the chance to bill Medicare for the procedure.

Every year thousands of men turn to their doctors to perform a mutilating procedure. It's said the notorious litterbug, Lorena Bobbitt, was trying the home method of this procedure—vasectomy.

After our second child was born, Diane and I discussed the two options of permanent birth control, and I lost. Although I still say she cheated on the tie-breaking arm wrestle.

In a visit to my doctor, who until that moment I had considered a friend, we were shown pictures of what the procedure involved. Diane seemed to enjoy them. I, on the other hand, sat in the fetal position in a corner with my hands over my ears singing, "La! La! La! I can't hear you!"

To make matters worse, the doctor produced a form for us to sign which, in effect, said that if Diane later got pregnant he couldn't be held liable. Does that sound as if he had faith in his ability? My veterinarian didn't make me sign a form saying he couldn't be held responsible if my dog had pups after he spayed it.

Then, at last, the appointed hour with the doctor came. I should have suspected something when it was after his regular office hours. He said it was to allow as much time as possible. My theory is that it was to avoid having other patients hear me scream.

Since all I was prepared for was "some minor discomfort," I had driven myself to his office. The only noticeable effect as I walked out was the feeling of suspended animation in that region of my anatomy.

Whenever my mouth is frozen at the dentist, it stays that way for hours, leaving me drooling and saying things like "I bond dink I can eab anyding pore dinner." The translation, of course, is: "I'll have the New York steak." My doctor must have bought cheap freezing, or watered it down. The freezing didn't slowly wear off; it shut off as if someone had flipped a switch—about five miles from home.

The other drivers sympathized. They left lots of room for the lunatic who was swerving and screaming. I tried hitting the brakes, but the sudden movement only made things worse, and I screamed again. Thankfully my doctor had given me a prescription to fill "just in case."

I pulled into the mall parking lot and was faced with a dilemma. How was I going to get out of the car? On my first attempt, I screamed louder than I had while driving. I even used the opportunity to try out a few words I had been saving for such an occasion. Women steered their small children away from my car.

"But, Mommy, the mall's that way!" one kid cried.

"I know, dear, but there's a man up there who sounds like your father did when the doctor fixed his pee-pee."

I finally made it to my feet and into the pharmacy, using a pace that was shuffle, stop, wince, curse. (I should have copyrighted the steps, because I now see people doing something similar on those dance shows country music networks air.) Then I presented the prescription to the female pharmacist.

The combination of female drugstore employees and anything to do with birth control has always been a source of embarrassment for men. This was no different. She looked at the prescription, then at me, and said in a voice that could be heard throughout the store, and by all the ships at sea, "Had a vasectomy, eh?"

At last I arrived home. My loving wife had the courtesy to turn her back as she was rocked with gales of laughter watching me try to get out of the car. One of my sons, in an attempt to comfort me, leaped onto my lap, knees first.

As I sat there, pills in hand, ice bag in crotch, I realized there had been a third possibility for permanent birth control—and celibacy sure sounded pretty good right about then.

I Need a Lot of Planning to Be Spontaneous

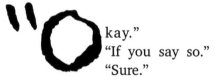"kay."

"If you say so."

"Sure."

I wish I could come up with quick-witted, spontaneous responses like those. So many other people can snap out such responses seemingly without a moment's hesitation.

When someone does or says something, I'm often stuck for the right response and end up babbling the first thing that comes to mind. When the bill arrives at a restaurant, my first reaction is to say, "Wait a second. You asked what you could get us. Doesn't that mean you're picking up the bill, too?"

It's often much later when I think, Gee, I could have come up with a quick riposte like "Thank you." I guess I'm just not very good at being spontaneous.

Diane's superiority in this department was evident once when we were driving through the mountains. We'd driven at least thirty miles since the last place, a gas station/snack bar/junk shop. Since neither of us felt like a chocolate bar for dinner—especially one that offered a chance to win a trip to the Olympic Games in Atlanta—we had continued along the twisting mountain roads. Finally, somewhere west of the middle of nowhere, we came upon a restaurant and hotel.

Diane went to get us a table, while I stopped at the gift shop to look at the genuine aboriginal carvings. These particular carvings were unique because the artist left the country to get the right materials to produce them. Either that or his name was "Made in Taiwan." Before I could make a decision between the bear holding a plastic thermometer or the wolf standing beside a pill bottle full of toothpicks, my wife returned.

Apparently the waitress had ignored Diane with her undivided attention. Finally, when she was sure the other eight or nine customers had full water glasses, the inventory of the cutlery was completed and the chairs were all neatly organized, she came to the entrance.

"Do you have a reservation?" she asked in a poor rendition of a Parisian accent.

Diane looked at the twenty-five or thirty empty tables and asked the waitress if many people driving through the mountains called ahead for reservations.

"Oh, yes," Miss Gallic Attitude replied. "We are *très* busy."

Despite being so busy, she managed to find room among the many invisible people who had called ahead for reservations. Unfortunately Diane made the mistake of telling her we weren't that hungry and just wanted to get some soup or a salad.

"Well, then, perhaps zee food and zee ambience of zee bar and pool room next door would suit you better."

Diane fired back one of her quick-witted, spontaneous remarks, clearly unconcerned about the waitress's feelings or the rules of polite conversation. "Oh, I see."

I was in awe. I forgot all about the carvings and followed Diane to "zee bar and pool room." "Zee ambience" came from the aroma of greasy burgers combined with the sight of several dead animal heads staring at us from every wall and the sound of bikers playing pool in the corner. As we waited for our mystery meals, Diane told me she was glad I hadn't been with her when she was dealing with the waitress at the first place. She knew I might have caused her great embarrassment because I wouldn't have thought of a quick comeback like "Oh, I see."

She's right. It would have taken a lot of careful planning for me to be that spontaneous. I might have thought up something appropriate an hour or two later, but my immediate responses would have been much louder and simpler:

- "Ambience? Where we come from that's what they drive you to the hospital in. Do we look sick or something?"
- "Ambience? Shoot, girl, we don't need no ambience. We haven't eaten the food here yet."
- "That's okay. I don't think I'll have an ambience, anyway, because I'm driving."
- "Are you saying all your other customers aren't good enough for the ambience of a pool hall so they have to eat here?"
- "If you'd been driving for seven hours, you'd be more suited to the ambience of a pool hall, too, sweetie."

I'll have to drive that same stretch of highway again someday. Now that I'm better prepared for spontaneity, I might stop back in to see if the waitress will give me a chance to say a great line like "Oh, I see."

Even if she doesn't, I can pick up that bear holding a thermometer. It'll go with the ambience in my office.

The Complaint Department Is Now Closed

A whole lot of complaining goes on in my house. I'm not sure who died and left me with the job of complaint-department supervisor, but I'm on the receiving end of a lot of whining, grumbling and protesting.

There's no worse time for young parents than when their firstborn is teething. Nothing will satisfy the child. He's cranky and generally unpleasant to be around—nothing like the sweet little bundle of joy they brought home from the hospital a few months earlier.

I thought that Diane and I were through all that trauma many years ago but, as is so often the case with parenting issues, I was wrong.

We thought eighteen-year-old Mike's surly mood a while ago stemmed from his impending graduation from high school, his eager anticipation of word from the college he applied to or just general teenage angst. We never considered he might be teething.

He expected to get some sympathy when he announced his mouth hurt due to a wisdom tooth erupting through the gums. He didn't realize he had used up his full quota of teething-related sympathy by the end of 1982.

His mother couldn't conjure up any sympathy for someone griping about his sore gums who was nearly a foot taller than she was. She didn't even try to hide her laughter at the thought of her six-foot-three little boy teething.

Mike was unimpressed with his mother, to say the least, but he knew better than to turn to me for parental support on this issue. I figured it was fate getting back at him for all the times he'd left me gnashing my teeth in the past eighteen years.

Mike wasn't the only one looking for sympathy, but not finding much. Diane expected some, too. When I'm woken up, I'm generally not in a sympathetic frame of mind. After more than twenty-five years of marriage, Diane should have realized that if she felt the need to tell me something in the middle of the night, I'd only be interested if it involved food, threats to my personal safety or food.

"Is it hot in here, or is it just me?" she asked at 11:15, 12:00, 1:05, 2:35, 3:10 . . .

"It's not hot in here," I told her through my sleep-craved haze. "It must just be you."

"Oh, I'm so hot," she announced at 11:20, 12:05, 1:10, 2:40, 3:15 . . .

My suggestion that she hold onto a pan full of muffin batter, so that we'd have something to eat at breakfast was not taken kindly. I couldn't twist my head around far enough to see if there was a bruise where she kicked me.

"My feet feel like they're on fire," she added at 11:25, 12:10, 1:15, 2:45, 3:20 . . .

"Don't worry," I said. "There are fresh batteries in the smoke detector. If your feet really do catch fire, we should have plenty of warning before the house is engulfed in flames."

"I can't understand why it's so hot in here," she said at 11:30, 12:15, 1:20, 2:50, 3:25 . . .

"It's not hot in here," I repeated. "In fact, since you've

opened the window so wide, I'm a little concerned about the possibility of hypothermia."

This went on throughout the night. I lost count of the number of times she complained about the heat, suggested that I might be cold-blooded and threw the blankets off both of us. I do know that I didn't get a heck of a lot of sleep.

For some reason, Diane thought that keeping me awake complaining about her temperature instability was justified by her claims that I snored.

Oh, sure I do.

What she was hearing was herself complaining about impending spontaneous combustion. I have never once heard myself snoring. Therefore, with no proof, I'd say she was making up these unfounded accusations about nocturnal noises I allegedly make.

I guess, in their own way, Mike and Diane turned to me because of my superior problem-solving capabilities. (Okay, they might have been complaining to me because there was no one else around, but I like to imagine I have superior problem-solving capabilities, so let me have my delusions of grandeur.) After much thought, I solved all their problems with a trip to the grocery store. I bought Mike a package of teething biscuits, and Diane a king-size ice pack. I took care of my own biggest complaint, too.

I bought myself some industrial-strength earplugs.

Yes, Dear

It's always nice to know I've been doing something right for more than twenty-five years.

I realize wives might find it a bit hard to accept that someone like me, who happens to be a husband, has done something right. I almost didn't believe it myself, but the proof was right on the front page of my newspaper a short while ago.

"Study Indicates 'Yes, Dear' Is Key to Wedded Bliss," read the headline. A subhead added: "Psychologists say husbands who agree with their wives have lasting marriages."

I've been married to Diane for more than a quarter century, and I think that fits into the category of a lasting marriage. I learned early that a well-placed, "Yes, dear" can do wonders.

In the news item, Tomas Maugh of the *Los Angeles Times*, wrote: "Husbands, forget all that psychobabble about active listening and validation. If you want your marriage to last for a long time, the newest advice from psychologists is quite simple: just do what your wife says."

He was paraphrasing the words of Dr. John Gottman of the University of Washington, who said that asking couples in the midst of conflict to use active-listening techniques was the equivalent of advocating emotional gymnastics.

For those who may have slept through the eighties, active listening was the technique that required one partner to reword what the other said. You were supposed to look into your partner's eyes, hold her hands and show her you really were a wonderful human being because you were trying to understand her concerns. Back then husbands often had a lot of trouble with that. Personally I thought the holding-hands rule was a good one. By holding Diane's hands, I saved myself from a lot of violence if I paraphrased inappropriately.

For example, when confronted with the statement "You really make me mad when you don't put your dirty clothes in the laundry basket," we were supposed to show our deep concern for our partners' feelings by saying something like "So what I hear you saying is you're feeling emotionally disturbed because I threw my socks in the corner and my underwear ended up hanging from the lamp shade."

We grew up hearing our fathers respond to our mothers with a variety of grunts that meant anything from "I know, I know, I know" to "Gimme a break." In reality, the only difference between that and active listening, was that with the latter we had to take the time to think up synonyms for what our wives said. The socks were still in the corner, the underwear was still hanging from a lamp shade and our wives were still choked because our Michael Jordan impersonations didn't get the stuff into the laundry basket. At least we could feel good about supposedly being better husbands because we were actively listening to their complaints.

About ten years ago or so, Diane and I went on a couple of those weekend retreats where they taught active listening. We really tried to use the skills, too, but putting it into practice was a lot harder than it sounded. More often than not, our active-listening sessions ended up with someone saying, "I know you're trying to say what you thought I said, but what I hear you saying isn't exactly what I meant to say when I said it, unless I'm not understanding what you think you're saying about what I said." Half the time we got so confused trying to paraphrase each other's statements that we forgot what we were originally talking about. Usually we wouldn't remember until the heat from the light bulb caused the underwear hanging from the lamp shade to smolder.

Then we'd start all over again.

Dr. Gottman is right. A simple "Yes, dear" is all that's really needed—together with bending down to pick up the socks in the corner, reaching over to extract the underwear from the lamp shade and depositing the whole lot into the laundry basket.

Let's face it, if Diane says, "I hate coming home to a mess," I can either say, "You appear to be saying that you get bent out of shape because our living room doesn't look like Martha Stewart's," or "Yes, dear." Which would be safer?

I can predict what Diane will say when she reads these words. It will be something like "When you write a column like this, you make me sound unreasonable for expecting you to put your laundry in the laundry basket every time."

Hey, what can I say? I'm a man. I've got to go with "Yes, dear" on that one.

Quelling a Taste for Champagne on a Tap-Water Budget

Every so often you need to do something to put yourself back in your place. Diane and I were feeling pretty good about ourselves. She was doing well at work, my newspaper column and magazine articles were selling in a lot more places and we'd found a way to take care of our debts legally. Overall, we were looking into the tunnel and seeing a light at the end of it, and it wasn't a train heading directly toward us.

Obviously we should have assumed we were looking into someone else's tunnel. Clearly it was time to snap ourselves back to reality. We needed to find something we wanted to buy that was so far out of our reach that we could start worrying about our impoverished state again.

So we went to an RV show.

For those who have never had the pleasure of attending one of these events, let me explain. An RV show brings together a variety of vehicles with prices that have six figures before the decimal place. Reading the price tag on a motor home could make someone much better off than

Diane and I are gasp. It can be quite humbling to kick the tires of a vehicle that costs more than the house we paid for just nine years ago. It's even more humbling to stare in wonder at an RV priced slightly higher than our estimated lifetime incomes. Some of them were bigger than the first two apartments Diane and I had lived in—combined.

One vehicle came with hardwood floors, solid wood paneling and furniture that looked as if it was better than anything we would ever consider having in our home. The only people I knew who had furniture that good were the kind who kept plastic over it and roped off the room that it was in. Somehow that didn't seem practical in something called a recreational vehicle.

I had looked at RVs as a slightly more civilized form of camping, which I've never been a big fan of. To me, roughing it means finding out there's no grapefruit juice in the morning, or that I'm not within a short driving distance of a really good cup of coffee. We discovered that RVs were to camping what the royal yacht *Britannia* was to canoeing. It only makes sense. Would you take your hardwood floors and fine furniture out to someplace where you might get pine needles in your shoes?

Apparently the idea is to leave your home in the suburbs and get away from it all by driving three hundred miles in a vehicle that uses a gallon of gas every four miles. You park it in something that looks just like the subdivision you left at home, except that all the houses have wheels and engines. The roads are paved, there is cable and satellite TV and the RV next door is closer to you than the house next door is back home. Many RVs come equipped with a device that lets you tow the family car so that, even though you're three hundred miles from home, you can still drive to a shopping mall that looks like the one down the road from your house.

It didn't take us too long to realize we were out of our league financially. We wandered around the hall for about an hour before we found anything we thought we might be able to afford, but neither of us felt like a cup of coffee right then. Just as well, at the price they were charging we'd have had to share a cup, and Diane only drinks decaf, so I wouldn't have enjoyed it, anyway.

Going to the RV show had its desired effect. We came to the conclusion that we had a lot better things to spend our money on than a motor home, and we weren't nearly so confident about our financial future as we had been before. We now know that the likelihood of us ever having the disposable income needed to own an RV dwindles more every time one of our sons comes home from school and says, "I need a new . . ."

Now that we have that out of our systems we can spend our evenings doing the things we do best—worrying about our finances, drafting and redrafting imaginary budgets that show us spending less than we earn and laughing when we imagine actually living that way.

Even if we do find that life is getting easier financially, we won't have to worry about it for long. The boat show is just around the corner.

Surviving Ground Zero
in the Nuclear Family

At Least We're Needed for Something

As parents, we all need to know we're important to our offspring. During the early years of childhood, our children obviously depend on us for just about everything. As they age, that dependency is supposed to ease when they spread their wings and seek their independence. Our usefulness in their lives becomes less important. Roles change. Where once children were to be seen and not heard, those same children now wish parents could be neither seen nor heard—unless there's some pressing need that only a parent can seemingly fill. Usually these involve money, food, transportation, food, clothing and, of course, food.

Diane and I finally discovered a way to determine if our two teenage sons needed us around all the time. We went away. It was gratifying to learn we weren't useless pains in their teenage butts. Despite what they were willing to admit, dear old Mom and Dad were still pretty useful to have around. You might even say we were downright vital.

My sons were forced to get by without my wife's nagging and were free of my unreasonable demands for an entire week. Not once during that time did they have to lis-ten to Diane ask them to bring their dirty dishes back to the kitchen. It must have been heavenly. In a normal week, they probably would have heard her nagging about those dishes somewhere in the neighborhood of 210 times. And they had seven days of absolute freedom from my insensitivity. They were able to watch reruns of *The Simpsons* in their entirety without being asked to help out around the house.

We tried to make sure most of their needs were attend-ed to during our absence. Friends took them in at dinner-time and rides were arranged for Mike to get to his night-school classes and for Brad to attend his hockey games and practices. We even stocked the fridge and pantry with a rea-sonable supply of edible products to sustain them through their after-school and after-dinner feeding frenzies.

We also left them each with a supply of cash to get them by should an emergency crop up. Naturally emergen-cies occurred. Brad was forced to go out and buy a couple of new videos. I'm thankful he had that money. If we hadn't given it to him, he might have had to use some of his own cash reserves for those videos, as well as for a few video-game rentals and comic books that were essential to his well-being during that week. Mike faced his share of emer-gencies, as well. That money proved to be the only thing that saved him from certain starvation. He might actually have had to make his own breakfast in the morning had we neglected to provide the financial means for him to buy the most important meal of the day.

Both boys were shocked that we weren't relieved we had provided for such emergencies. In their minds, it was pretty unreasonable for us to assume there might be some, if not all, of that money left at the end of the week, since the house hadn't burned to the ground, the refrigerator hadn't given up the ghost and they hadn't needed to buy any new school supplies. They really shouldn't have been that shocked. After all, their mother and I clearly had a pretty outdated view about what was and what wasn't an emergency expenditure.

We even flew the boys to Toronto to join us on the last days of my Ontario tour to promote my column. Naturally we were worried about the state of the house. Would there be piles of moldy dishes sitting around waiting for the dish fairy to clean? Did the cats' litter boxes get changed during our absence? Did the garbage get taken out? Will the vacuum cleaner have seen any action? Will the inside of the microwave be caked with the remnants of exploded pizza snacks?

We didn't get reassuring, confidence-building answers to those and many similar questions. I was relieved to know that I would be flying home twenty-four hours after my wife, thereby avoiding having to testify in any court case that might result from her discovery of the condition of the kitchen. Diane vocalized her own misgivings before she left.

"Perhaps," she said, "I'll just stay away rather than return to a mountain of housework."

"But," cried Mike, "you have to come home. There are no clean dishes!"

It's so nice to feel needed.

I'm Supporting a Pair of Walking Dichotomies

If today's teenagers want understanding, why do they make themselves so difficult to understand?

My sons, Mike and Brad, think we don't understand them and, well, they're right. I'm supporting a pair of walking contradictions. For every action, they seem to have an equal or greater inactivity. For example:

- The son who set a provincial record in power skating can take twenty minutes to cover the distance from his bedroom to the kitchen when it's his turn to set the table
- The teenager who can explain the inner workings of a computer can't figure out how to use a plunger when he plugs the toilet
- The boy who can pass a hockey puck to a teammate forty feet away and have it arrive right on the other player's stick can't hit a laundry basket with a T-shirt from three feet
- The teenager who can calculate pi to multiple decimal places in his head can't determine that the left-

over pie in the fridge is meant for dessert, not an after-school snack

- The son who can remember the unusual names of every character in the *Star Wars* trilogy can't remember to flush the toilet unless I happen to be in the shower at the time
- The boy who can successfully search for all kinds of information on the Internet can't take down a name or telephone number when I get a call

With dichotomies like those, is it any wonder their mother and I don't understand them?

Of course, the whole problem is our fault. Now that we're in our forties, we fit somewhere in the middle of the socioeconomic group—boomers—that's to blame for all the world's problems. We're regularly told how much better the world would be if these dreaded boomers hadn't messed everything up. We get blamed for everything from pollution to the national debt. That's odd, because I was sure those things were my parents' fault.

I take exception to being blamed for pollution by people who are responsible for some of the biggest sources of environmental degradation themselves. I'm convinced that the hole in the ozone layer is a direct result of air escaping from minor-hockey dressing rooms and equipment bags. Nipper, our cocker spaniel, even tries to hold her breath if she has to walk past Brad's hockey bag. My wife swears something growled at her the last time she tried to unload the bag in a search for missing socks, towels and underwear. I think it would be cheaper to replace the missing clothes than to pay for the damage they could do to the washing machine, our plumbing and all ocean life within two hundred miles of shore.

I firmly believe my hair is going prematurely gray because of the overexposure to postgame sweat I've had to endure. In order to save myself from going completely gray,

I've taken to driving home from Brad's games with my head out the side window. The fumes from diesel engines are sweet perfume in comparison to the aroma emanating from the sweaty body in the passenger seat.

My older son, Mike, once convinced us to allow him to keep a hamster in his bedroom. The smell in his room was awful, but the hamster eventually got used to it. I'm afraid to venture too far into that room. I think there might be several new life-forms developing their own civilizations in the dirty dishes and forgotten half-full glasses of milk he has in there.

Another form of environmental disregard constantly perpetrated by my sons comes in the form of wasted energy. There is an apparent misunderstanding about the two-way function of light switches and television power buttons. They have mastered the ability to turn on the lights and the television, but it seems they haven't figured out how to turn them off again.

On average, between my wife and me, we turn the hall, stairwell, dining room and kitchen lights off four or five times—after we go to bed. Each time one of the boys needs to restock his bedroom food supply, he has to turn on all the lights. They stay lit long after the culprit returns to his room. Eventually the light shining under our bedroom door wakes one of us up and we groggily take a tour of the house turning things off. On a positive note, we recently got a card from the airport thanking us for providing such a well-lit landmark for pilots on foggy nights.

Seven Per Cent
of a Whale of a Time

So here I am in the middle of that great traditional institution and sanity challenge known as the family vacation. I have just spent $300 so that my nuclear family can go out onto a genuine ocean searching for bona fide whales.

I have two theories about why they call parents and their children a nuclear family. My personal belief is that compressing two teenagers into the family car or a single hotel room bed can cause a massive explosion if one touches the other. The scientific school of thought by the people who coined the phrase has something to do with the immediate blood relationship of the family members. This theory is easily refuted in my family because I am only related to my wife by marriage.

We are two hundred miles from home. A meager twenty miles from our house is an aquarium featuring two real live, in the flesh, killer whales waiting there to be marveled at by the general public. All that marveling can be done while you're standing on solid ground.

My family wanted to experience whales in their natural habitat. Fearing that one, or both, of my nuclear sons would have a core meltdown without this experience, I relented . . . again.

As we pulled into the parking lot, the wind suddenly picked up speed as if nature were sending us a signal that whales are only to be viewed from the gallery of the aquarium. Heading out to sea wasn't to be considered lightly. Looking at the waves brought to mind those three little words that mean so much: *small-craft warning*.

After the obligatory hundred-dollar visit to the gift shop, we were herded onto what looked like an awfully tiny boat. On board with us was a lady from Seattle, a couple from Holland and forty-five French-Canadian senior citizens. English was at a premium.

The weather started getting rough.
The tiny ship was tossed.
If not for a dose of some Gravol pills,
Our lunches would be lost.

Most of the French Canadians spent the entire trip huddled inside the boat. They kept saying things like *"Tabernacle Chevrolet coupe avec wire wheels,"* which I believe, thinking back on my high school French, means "Bring me the head of John the travel agent."

After about a half hour of pitching and tossing, we saw an authentic pod of killer whales. To be perfectly truthful, we saw some whale fins and tails. This awe-inspiring sight lasted a full twenty minutes and left us wondering what we would be doing for the remainder of the five-hour cruise.

The captain thought he knew where the whales might have gone and sent us bouncing over six-foot waves trying to catch up with them. Several of the French Canadians had obviously developed a rapport with one of the whales. They were hanging over the rails calling him by his first name. Despite many calls of "Ohhhh, Rrrraaaalllph," the whales eluded us. Mind you, if I was the whale I wouldn't have answered them, either. The way they were pronouncing his name sounded remarkably like they were throwing up.

We were told the whales had undoubtedly entered Robson Bight. I made the suggestion that we follow them there.

"Can't," said the captain.

"Why not?" I asked, having clearly missed some of the subtle inferences and nuances of his detailed answer.

"Boats aren't allowed in there. It's been set aside to give the whales some privacy."

"So what you're saying is that we've spent $75 a person to see whales for approximately seven per cent of the cruise time because the whales have gone in there and closed the curtains so that they can privately do whatever it is that we paid to see whales do," I said, trying hard not to have my own nuclear meltdown.

"Well," he said, "there's also the dinner we'll be serving you once we get behind that island and into calmer water."

Dinner was served and actually eaten by some of the passengers. At the thought of eating, several more French Canadians thought it might be useful to lean over the rail and try to make contact with Ralph the whale again. Dinner consisted of a bowl of luke-cold soup, a sandwich and two cookies. Any fool could see it was easily a $70 dinner.

As we sailed back to port, I saw a couple on the shore of an island walking along hand in hand. I could have sworn it was Gilligan and Mary Ann. I always knew those two would get it together.

On the way back to the hotel, I had a feeling I was being watched by Greenpeace, because we were only five miles from the parking lot when one of my sons touched the other, setting off another nuclear-family explosion.

Strike Camping Off My "To Do" List

Each summer Brad and I spend a week at the Okanagan Hockey School in Penticton, British Columbia. As his personal driver, I always get to go along.

In past years, while Brad slept in the air-conditioned comfort of the dormitory, the rest of the family camped. On the last trip, I sought out the comforts of a bed-and-breakfast because I had sworn off camping for good the previous year. It had involved a discovery I'd made as I'd lain in my sleeping bag trying to find a spot where the rain wasn't dripping through the waterproof tent—I hate camping.

I realize there are people out there who enjoy camping, cooking over an open fire and wondering if a black widow spider just bit them behind the ear. These are the people who can pitch a tent in gale-force winds and start a fire by scratching two rocks together. These are the ones who actually enjoy picking bits of soot out of their eggs in the morning.

I had camped with my family when I was a child. My father's way of doing it usually involved driving for several hours to "rough it" in a trailer. His idea of roughing it meant he could only get one television channel, and that was if I held the antenna.

I had never camped on my own before the summer of my revelation, though. In previous years, other members of my nuclear family had been responsible for things like setting up the tent, starting the fires and picking the soot out of my eggs before I could see it. That summer of my last camping experience I had hoped Brad would help me get the tent set up, but he had to be at the hockey school before I could get a campsite.

I never knew how entertaining it could be setting up a tent by myself. I entertained the entire campground as they sat and watched me try to balance on my crutches and struggle to insert pin A into hole B on post 1. When I moved to the opposite side to repeat the process, the first pin A would slip out of its hole B. While correcting that, of course, the second hole B disgorged its pin A and so on and so on.

I was beginning to think I had a paraplegic tent, because every time I got it to stand, it would fall over. I was ready to give up and sleep in the van when a member of my audience came over. He showed a keen sense of the obvious.

"Looks like y'all are havin' trouble with that thang," he pointed out. "Used to have one like this before I got me the RV." A quick motion with his thumb indicated the rusting hulk of what was once a yellow school bus. "Any fool can get one up in no time, but I guess you bein' a cripple an' all . . ."

I'm not noted for being overly politically correct, but "cripple" is one of those terms that makes me cringe every time I hear it, especially if it's used to describe me. I had an urge to smack him silly with one of the uncooperative tent poles. I tempered that idea because, even though he had consumed several cans of beer while watching me fight with the tent, he was probably just the kind of fool who could set the thing up.

All I wanted to do as soon as the tent was erect was to

climb into my sleeping bag and collapse. I thought it was a good omen that none of the area's rattlesnakes or black widow spiders had taken up residence in the sleeping bag before I had a chance to. I just hoped they'd refrain from joining me later.

I awoke in the middle of the night to the sound of rain beating against the tent and the wind blowing heavily against the sides. The rain was also falling fairly heavily inside the tent because the zipper on the window had zipped its last zip.

If you tell anyone you're going camping, they'll always pass on the same advice—don't touch the tent during a rainstorm. When I awoke, I sat up and broke this cardinal camping rule, thus giving the rain more routes to my sleeping bag.

When my wife, the career Girl Guide, arrived at the end of the week, she was able to tell me all the things I had done wrong. I enjoyed her commentary so much that I was tempted to show my appreciation by doing something that would have been illegal, immoral and a surefire trip to divorce court.

I found some satisfaction in vowing I would commit myself if I ever had the slightest urge to go camping again.

Send in the Clones

Mary had a little lamb,
A scientist made its clone.
Soon kids will want to be the first
With themselves to call their own.

'm thinking of having myself cloned, but my ever-supportive wife doesn't think the world is ready for that yet. We've recently learned that scientists have perfected the technique by cloning a sheep, a monkey and a kosher smoked meat on rye with extra pickles. Can humans be far behind?

Ever since Dolly, the sheep in lamb's cloning, made her appearance, every newspaper, magazine and television news program has focused on the negative issues surrounding the ethics of cloning. She's also caused an eruption of letters to the editor. The majority of them say cloning is baa-aaa-d.

These people haven't had time to think about the advantages of cloning someone in the image of yourself. The prospects are limitless, especially at my house.

Hopefully someone will see the entrepreneurial possibilities and open a chain of One-Hour Clone-Developing

Centers. We'll just have to drop off our rolls of exposed Kodaclone, and voilà—instant duplicates with free reprints on Tuesdays. They could even offer enlargements for people who need a bigger clone to clean the gutters.

I plan on giving my first clone all my duties as the indentured servant around my house. He'll drive those members of my family who find it difficult to walk the three blocks to their school. He'll also be called upon to drive to hockey practices at 3:45 in the morning.

Gordon 2 will also do the grocery shopping, which will totally absolve me of any blame when, even after spending $500 at the store, there's never anything good to eat in the house. And he can clean up the kitchen after each of my two sons eats—in one day—three meals, three after-school snacks, three after-dinner snacks and three late-night refrigerator snacks. Apparently, after expending so much energy getting themselves all the way to the kitchen and making twelve-course meals for themselves, their bodies are too drained of energy to throw out any garbage they've created or put away the remnants of the bread, butter, cheese, meat, ketchup . . .

Gordon 2 will have to set his alarm an hour earlier than mine so he can clean up the mess they leave behind when getting a little something in the middle of the night.

All of this mass destruction to our grocery budget can't be contained in the kitchen alone. Who in their right mind would think about eating a twelve-course snack at the table? That might be okay for some anal-retentive parents, but everyone knows that the only place to eat is in front of the television. When it's time to return to the kitchen for the next round of mayhem, they mustn't waste any of their precious energy doing stupid things like carrying the dishes, glasses, cutlery and leftovers back to the kitchen.

It might be amazing to learn that teenagers still believe in elves but, since the dish elf always takes care of that job for them, why not believe? Apparently our dish elf is getting pretty fed up with the workload he has around here, so perhaps we should think about having him replicated. His clone will have to be strong enough to lift a dessert bowl with a single hand and still have the stamina to rinse it and put it in the dishwasher. The dish elf will have to teach his body double how to find the Home of the Misplaced Snacks by sniffing out the glasses of curdled milk hidden behind the drapes, or plates shoved under the sofas. As a clone, he won't worry about the ethics of wiping out these miniature Gardens of Eden when he finds them teeming with their own new forms of life.

There might be a slight disadvantage to having my duplicate around the house. With all the extra time I'd have, I could go off doing things I don't have time for now. I might return unexpectedly one day and find my wife and my best clone . . .

No doubt the rest of my family will want their own clones when they see how much mine does for me. The boys would want theirs to attend school for them and do the chores they don't do now. Hopefully their clones wouldn't be so identical that they would want to sit in front of the television or play computer games instead of cleaning out the kitty-litter box or mowing the lawn.

There's just one nagging thought that worries me about the boys getting cloned. Would I have to feed Mike 2 and Brad 2, too?

Gamesmanship
in the Nineties

I took Brad and a group of his friends to one of those indoor arcade/miniature golf complexes. The place offered free admission. Good thing they did, because their machines gobbled up $90 in tokens in less than two and a half hours. Add to that $30 for everyone to play miniature golf, and the words "affordable family fun center" seemed somewhat out of place.

I watched as the boys battled aliens, evildoers and supercharged, double-overhead cam, bionic robots with dual exhausts. One game turned them into gunfighters. They were like little Dr. Deaths of the Old West, assisting in the suicides of multitudes of bank robbers, horse thieves, cattle rustlers and innocent townsfolk who looked as if they might have a gun hidden in their bustles.

Since the boys were keeping themselves alive against this onslaught of terror, I naturally assumed it would be even easier for me. To put it simply, I assumed wrong.

These machines must have some kind of adult-detector system built into them. If a kid is playing the game, it cooperates. If an adult is playing, the little man in the game commits suicide as soon as he sees one of the bad guys. It's awfully disconcerting to have your man keel over at the sight of a mushroom, or jump off a cliff when a turtle strolls along.

My son was quite helpful. He was rather patronizing, though, when he said, "You're really doing quite well . . . for an adult." It was the same tone I used years ago, saying things like "Don't worry. Lots of people need mouth-to-mouth resuscitation during their first swimming lesson."

He told me I should jump to avoid being killed by the mushrooms and turtles. While I appreciated his advice, I found it difficult to concentrate on the game or the control button while jumping up and down in front of the machine.

My sons have a fairly substantial arcade of their own. Between game systems and their computers there must be about a hundred games in the house. I don't play with these often; I already have enough ways to humiliate myself.

One day Brad brought out his entire begging-and-guilt arsenal to get me to try a new game. I listened to everything from "It's really cool, Dad. You have to try it." to "In some countries it's the law that fathers play with their sons." Finally, after I reached the overweight-luggage counter on the guilt trip he was sending me on, I succumbed and agreed to play the "Way cool go-cart race game."

As I sat down at his computer, he reassured me by saying, "It's really easy, Dad. Even you should be able to make it work."

It's so nice to be thought of so highly. I had to agree, though. What could be easier than aiming a little cart and driver around a track on the screen? I quickly discovered that developing cold nuclear fusion would be easier.

There was only one speed. The police don't have vehicles that move at that pace. I'm not even sure NASA does. I drove my driver straight into a wall. Luckily he bounced off so that I could bash him into the wall again . . . and again . . . and again.

Brad finally leaped to his feet and saved the poor guy.

With a quick push of a couple of buttons, he was back on the road again, heading straight for a banana peel. (One of the other drivers was clearly a litterbug.) Suddenly something flashed past me on the road. Either this flash or the banana peel sent my car careening off a signpost and a pile of tires, leaving me driving the wrong way around the track. Brad explained that it was another driver who had lapped me.

"Boy, he must be a really fast driver," I said, still trying to find a way to get turned around.

"No, Dad," Brad said, barely able to hide his disappointment in my go-cart-driving ability. "That was the one driven by the hippopotamus. The fast drivers lapped you while you were trying to give your driver whiplash crashing into the wall back at the first curve."

I was beginning to think he had stumbled on the simulator used in most of the driving schools in this area, because it closely resembled our rush-hour traffic. Luckily, before somebody had the chance to rear-end my desk chair, "Game Over" flashed on the screen.

All was not lost. Brad eventually found a game for me. If I push the F1 key, it tells the computer to "Go Fish!"

Things That Go Gznork in the Night

Things that go bump in the night bother some people. I'm awakened each night by a repertoire of noises that occur, with measurable regularity, around Chez Kirkland. Few of them could be described as bumps.

One source of these noises is my son, Mike. Atomic bombs in his bedroom wouldn't wake him in the morning, but he's often still up well after midnight. He doesn't see there might be a correlation between the time he goes to bed and his inability to regain consciousness before the third class of the day.

Because he finds it so difficult to get himself out of bed in time to do anything other than throw on his clothes, raid my dresser because he can't find his own socks and spend fifteen minutes begging to be driven the three blocks to school, he has decided he should shower at night. This is done in the shower next door to our bedroom rather than the smaller one near his, and well after his mother and I have settled down for our long winter's nap.

Showering doesn't involve quietly stepping into the tub, gently closing the doors and turning the water on. He has to crash, bang and scream as that first jet of cold water leaves the shower head. Naturally, when finished showering, it's time to run a bath. For the next twenty minutes, I'm serenaded by the noise of wet skin against wet porcelain.

We are usually met with a scene of mass destruction in the washroom the next morning, because picking up towels, the bath mat and dirty clothes is against Mike's better principles. Unfortunately one of our miscreant cats has decided that the bath mat is gentler on her paws than the kitty-litter box, and we are also met with a little surprise from her.

Of course, when a teenage boy is awake, he's hungry. I'm sure if we served him an entire side of beef he'd still be starving a half hour later. One night he was dying from a severe case of malnutrition at 12:30 a.m. Those three hot dogs he'd had at 10:30 p.m. weren't enough to sustain him through the night.

Like showering, raiding the refrigerator is a sonic event. Cupboard doors, drawers, plates, glasses and cutlery must be banged, crashed, dropped and kicked. There's also the call of the famished teenager—"Why is there never any food in this house?"

Soon after the house becomes quiet, the next strange noises begin. When you're in a semiconscious state, these sounds can stir the imagination into believing that either the room has been filled with an entire flock of banshees or the title character in *The Texas Chain Saw Massacre* has dropped by for a visit. When I become fully awake, I realize that Diane is partaking in her nocturnal hobby—snoring, grinding her teeth and making fearful noises during a bad dream.

It becomes a chorus when Nipper, the dumbest dog ever to get lost on a single flight of stairs, joins in with snores, whimpers and barks in her sleep. She has decided to lay claim to a corner of our bed, which creates the illusion of surround-sound when the two of them get going.

On one occasion, I found myself suddenly pulled into

consciousness. It quickly became clear I was in my darkened bedroom, not frolicking on a beach with a bevy of super-models. My dear wife was sitting up in bed, shouting, "Oh, my gosh!"

One side of my brain was still wondering where Pamela Anderson had gone while the other was trying to remember the rules for coherent speech, resulting in something along the lines of "Yes, that's the . . . where are you . . . what the heck are you talking about?"

Diane stared at me and asked, "What do you mean?" then promptly went back to sleep.

I spent the next three hours staring at the ceiling and wondering what could possibly have happened that caused her to shout something that was actually a little bluer than "Oh, my gosh!" in the middle of the night.

Just moments before the alarm went off, I came to the only satisfactory conclusion. Prior to her shout, she had seen the disturbing image of a grocery clerk push the Total button for two grocery carts full of another week's groceries to feed the boys.

How Do They Park in a Parallel Universe?

After months of fear and trepidation, my oldest son, Mike, finally got his driver's license. The fear and trepidation belonged to Diane and me, especially when we had to go out with him while he practiced. For the most part, I left that job to my wife, although she gave me an important duty to take care of while she and Mike were out driving. I was in charge of hosing down the driveway every day. She wanted the ground she'd be kissing to be clean when she got home.

So now the trouble really begins. We have no plans to buy him a car. He is restricted to occasional use of his mother's ten-year-old Honda—definitely not something that fits into the category of cool cars. We're having a little difficulty teaching Mike the principles of financial thermal dynamics. That's the scientific term for paying for the gas he burns to drive the car.

He picked up a rather annoying habit when using my car, though. I can ignore the pleading that goes on whenever I get into the driver's seat. It's a trick I learned from my father, who ignored my pleas about driving his car until three years after I was married. Since getting his license,

Mike has been behind the wheel of my car twice. On both occasions, he drove it down the driveway and parked it at the curb so that he could get his mother's car out of the carport.

For the life of me, I can't quite understand why, for a drive of that distance, he needs to change the radio station and crank up the volume. During the time it takes him to park the car on the street, he could only have been subjected to, at most, one verse of a song on the station I listen to. Odds are he got to listen to half of a commercial on the alternative rock station he favors. One thing's for sure, he was able to hear it. When I start my car after these little drives of his, people in China can probably hear the radio.

He was able to get his license even though he didn't do well on the parallel-parking part of his driving test. However, he won't tell me what he did wrong.

"I don't want to read about it in his next column," he said when Diane asked him to tell me why he hadn't passed parallel parking.

He swore his mother to secrecy, and so far I haven't been able to get her to tell me. Therefore, I'll just have to guess, won't I? There are a number of things that could result in a failing grade in parallel parking. I can only assume he made one of the classic driver's-test faux pas.

For example, he could have turned parallel parking into a twenty-minute workout. Lots of people who have licenses demonstrate this habit—usually right in front of me. I've sat waiting while drivers have gone through as many as twelve attempts at getting their cars into a roadside parking space. Perhaps they might have found it easier if I hadn't been blaring my horn through attempts seven to twelve.

I'm sure Mike might have had difficulty convincing the instructor he knew how to parallel park if he'd brought the car up to about a hundred kilometers per hour (sixty miles per hour for the metrically challenged), hit the brakes and pulled the steering wheel hard to the left, thus executing a perfect sideways skid into the parking spot. Driving examiners don't tend to give extra points for artistic merit.

I certainly hope they wouldn't have passed him if he used the tactile method of parallel parking. I know it's quite common. I have the marks on the front and rear bumpers of my car to prove how often people determine their location in a parking space by the feel of their car hitting the one behind or in front of it. One of these days I expect to return to my car and find that my air bags have been activated by an overzealous tactile parallel parker.

I can't be too hard on Mike about parallel parking. His mother says he's actually been quite good at it when she's been with him while he practiced. That's really quite high praise. She's almost completely lost the facial tic she developed while trying to teach him when and where to apply the brakes. I have to admit that parallel parking is something I try to avoid if at all possible. I use the two-space-or-drive method. If there aren't at least two adjoining spaces so that I can drive right into one of the spots, I keep driving.

But I'm not going to tell Mike that. I don't want to read about it in his next English composition.

Is There an Overreaders Anonymous?

I suppose it's our fault.

Parents have to take responsibility for the way their offspring turn out, so I guess we're the only ones to blame for the habit our son, Brad, has developed.

He reads.

How on earth did we ever stray so far from society's standards? Our son would actually rather read a book than deal drugs, father a child with one of his teachers or get together with his buddies for an evening's indulgence in the youthful joy that only a smash-and-grab robbery or a carjacking can deliver. At this rate, Diane and I will never get invited to talk about him on television with Jerry Springer, Montel Williams or Sally Jessy Raphaël.

I think I know where we went wrong. It all started with those darn Dr. Seuss books. Even today, so many years later, I can't see a turtle in a pet store without thinking about "the far away Island of Salamasond" where "Yertle the Turtle was king of the pond." I must have read Brad that story about the "nice little pond" where "it was clean, it was neat, the water was warm, there was plenty to eat" a thousand times.

Yertle the Turtle isn't the only book from that era I can

still recite by heart. There's *Horton Hears a Who*, *How the Grinch Stole Christmas*, a dozen Berenstain Bear books, a huge collection featuring the escapades of Mickey Mouse, Donald Duck and Goofy and, of course, *Winnie-the-Pooh and the Blustery Day*. Yet despite this incredible memory for the words to children's books I read twelve or thirteen years ago, I can't remember what my wife asked me to get at the grocery store twenty minutes ago.

I should have realized Brad was becoming a problem overreader when, sprinkled in and among the computer games on his Christmas list, he requested books. Books? That was always the gift that ranked right up there with socks and underwear.

Some people might not think having an overreader is much of a problem in the greater scheme of things. Sure, we aren't being awakened by telephone calls from the police at three in the morning to be told our son has been involved in a drive-by reading. No angry fathers are pounding on our door accusing our son of statutory reading to their daughters. He's not likely to get shot in a book deal gone bad.

Parents of problem overreaders live in their own special self-made hell. Requests for help around the house by normal parents might elicit a response suggesting they get stuffed (or something meaning the same thing, but using more colorful language, sprinkled with several "likes" and "y'knows") Lately, when we ask Brad to set the table or some other equally mundane activity, he unabashedly tells us to wait until he's finished the page he's reading.

You can imagine how that makes us feel.

It's especially frustrating when, twenty minutes later, dinner is ready, the table is still not set and he's still goofing off reading a book. I could understand if he was out hanging around the entrance of a 7-Eleven store like normal kids, but he tries to excuse his lack of assistance by saying, "You really can't expect me to stop in mid-sentence, Dad, and once I start a new page, I have to finish it and the one on the right-hand side of the book, too."

It's probably my fault for never stopping in the middle of *Yertle the Turtle*.

Like the parents of overreaders everywhere, I'm concerned about the effect all this reading is having on him. While I can be somewhat thankful he isn't reading pornography or how-to manuals for home nuclear bomb construction, I'm still worried about some of his choices of what he is, and isn't, willing to read. I wish he would expand his love of reading beyond books and magazines.

Sure, it might not be as exciting as battles on some distant planet, but I'd like to see him start reading more important things. It's not as if I'm asking him to read William Shakespeare, John Keats or Rudyard Kipling, but I would be happy if he read the instructions on a package of microwavable popcorn.

If he did that, my own overreading habit might not be punctuated by the sounds of the smoke detector, the sight of scorched popcorn being extinguished in the kitchen sink and the smell of burning artificial butter-flavored additive.

Legal Interpretations for Parents of Teenagers

I've been doing some legal research lately. I wanted to make sure my sons can't sue their mother and me at some point in the future, and I've learned quite a bit that might prove useful to others in my situation.

Readers will be pleased to know that asking a teenager to set and/or clear the table doesn't constitute an affront to their civil liberties. The federal, state and provincial legislative bodies in North America haven't found cause to include table setting in the definition of abusive behavior on the part of parental units. You needn't feel guilty for expecting the person given the responsibility of removing the dirty dishes from the table to ensure they get rinsed before they're put into the dishwasher. Believe it or not, you can feel justified in believing the full definition of this chore includes dealing with the cutlery. If your indentured teenagers toss the cutlery into the sink, assuming they actually survive the brutal chore of carrying it to the kitchen, you can ask them to complete the job without fearing charges of child abuse.

Bribery laws don't mention anything about parents expecting teenagers to carry out certain basic household functions if they want to be chauffeured to and from their after-school jobs, sports events or the mall. Telling a teenager you expect him to clean out the kitty-litter box before you'll drive him anywhere doesn't meet the requirements for consideration as a cruel and unusual punishment. In fact, the length of time it takes to get said adolescent to clean out the kitty-litter box could provide you with just cause for laying charges of environmental pollution and cruelty to animals.

Your offspring can't charge you with neglect if you fail to provide them with an endless supply of pop, chips, cookies, pre-made burgers and extra-large pizzas. Using the refrigerator to store useless items—fresh fruit, vegetables and the like—won't run you afoul of the law. Contrary to the beliefs of many people between the ages of thirteen and nineteen, serving vegetables as part of the evening meal doesn't violate any section of the US Constitution or the Canadian Charter of Rights.

Failure to provide enough sandwich meat for their 1:00 a.m. feeding frenzy and their lunch the next day isn't an indictable offense. It isn't even emotional abuse if you suggest that, since they ate all the luncheon meat in the middle of the previous night, perhaps they could take a peanut butter sandwich to school.

There are no laws in any of the G7 countries that say a parent must risk life and limb trying to retrieve dirty laundry from a teenager's bedroom. This fact absolves parents of the responsibility for knowing where clean clothes are hidden. The only clean underwear parents need to worry about the emergency room staff seeing is their own. You needn't fear any legal ramifications if your children arrive at school or the hospital wearing mismatched socks.

There is no crime in setting a limit on towel use. Most teenagers can eventually struggle through the effort of drying themselves with fewer than five towels. It doesn't even violate the child labor laws if you expect them to take their dirty clothes and towels to the laundry hamper instead of leaving them on the bathroom floor.

Hiding your teenager's coat on a hanger in the closet— instead of leaving it in the convenient location he put it on the floor beside the front door—doesn't constitute theft.

Teenagers don't receive any special treatment under the terms and conditions of the Geneva Convention. While it does protect prisoners of war and makes sure they receive the necessities of life, it doesn't specify that teenage prisoners of their parents' old-fashioned ways should receive the necessities of life such as cars, private telephone lines and unlimited credit at the video store.

There are no laws that allow teenagers to cite precedents created when other teenagers' parents cave in. The fact that Peter's parents presented him with a car in no way obligates the parents of every teenager remotely acquainted with Peter to do the same thing.

All this research has put my mind at ease. No matter how emotionally upsetting it might have been, my son has no legal recourse against me because I wasn't available to drive him home from work the other day. Forcing a teenager to put up with the indignities of taking a bus might seem cruel, but it is actually legal.

How High's the Water, Papa?

I don't think it would be unreasonable to say that my sons are strong-willed. After all, that's just a polite way of saying "stubborn as mules." Even with their ability to guard their opinions as though they've been given their supreme knowledge by a divine being speaking to them from a flaming shrub, I don't think they can come close to the test of wills my friend Roger's son attempted a while ago.

Had he been successful, it would have been a really neat trick. No one has tried it since Canute, England's Danish king, failed nearly a thousand years ago.

He tried to turn back the tide.

It didn't work.

Roger and I have often commiserated over the trials and tribulations of being the parents of teenagers. More often than not, he's been the one listening to me express amazement at the creative stubbornness shown by my sons. On this occasion, it was my turn to be the listener.

Like me, Roger has recently gone through the stresses of having a teenager learn to drive. He's been there before, so he knew what to expect. During the time when my son, Mike, was getting his license, Roger often smiled knowingly when I described the terrors I was experiencing. Still, I don't think anything could have prepared Roger for the events that unfolded with his son behind the wheel.

Roger owns, well, okay, to use the accurate tense, he "owned" a nearly new four-wheel-drive sport-utility truck. Everyone knows four-wheel drive can take you anywhere, anytime, and make you completely impervious to the hazards that might befall someone in a lesser vehicle. Neither rain, nor mud, nor sleet, nor snow can disturb a boy in a four-by-four. Apparently Roger's son was convinced of that fact when he decided to take a drive along the beach.

There wasn't rain. There wasn't mud. There wasn't sleet. There wasn't snow. There was, however, soft, wet beach sand in an area below the high-water line. Amazingly, soft, wet beach sand can indeed stop a four-by-four in its tracks. In fact, it's quite possible for one to get nicely stuck.

And that's exactly what happened to Roger's son.

The ocean has a peculiar habit every twelve hours or so. It's called high tide. The tide was out when the boy went for his drive. It was still out when he got stuck. It was out when they finally managed to get the vehicle towed from its spot on the beach. Unfortunately, between the time when the truck got stuck and the tow truck pulled it free, high tide came, washed over the vehicle and receded again.

When Roger arrived on the scene, the damage had been done. The Pacific Ocean had risen. All he could see was the roof and a bit of the windshield. The rest of his nearly new four-wheel-drive sport-utility truck was impersonating a waterlogged submarine.

To his credit, the boy had had the good sense to call a tow truck. Unfortunately there was a locked gate between the road and the beach. These events occurred on Good Friday. There was no one available to unlock the gate until it was too late. Roger never explained how his son managed to avoid the problem of the locked gate in getting to the beach in the first place, but I guess, being a teenager, he knew more than the tow-truck driver.

"It's totaled," Roger said with a note of parental resignation in his voice. "The salt water got into everything."

Like King Canute before him, all the boy could do was watch the tide ignore his will and make its run to the high-water line. Legend tells us that old Canute was trying to demonstrate that even a king couldn't stop the rising tide, but I'm sure, deep down, he was pretty ticked off at the disobedient sea. Still, whatever the king thought, I'm certain it couldn't compare with the emotions Roger's son felt as the tide slowly slipped over the hood of his dad's nearly new four-wheel-drive sport-utility truck.

I'd be willing to bet that the whole story of King Canute has been altered over the passage of time. Maybe he was a teenager when he tried to command the tide to stay out. Perhaps he had gotten his father's nearly new four-wheel wagon stuck in the soft, wet beach sand. I wonder if he got grounded for life, too.

It kind of puts leaving the gas tank empty into perspective, doesn't it?

I'll Take Secondhand Smoke over Secondhand Sweat Any Day

S ome time ago I spent a weekend in the home of the world's most famous secondhand smoke.

Whistler, British Columbia, is the ski resort town that Olympic gold medal snowboarder Ross Rebagliati calls home. During the 1998 Winter Olympics in Nagano, Japan, Rebagliati was briefly stripped of his medal because he had traces of marijuana in his bloodstream. He was later able to appeal the decision successfully, claiming that inhaling secondhand smoke at his send-off party was the only way marijuana could be in his system.

Coincidentally, that weekend, Whistler was hosting three better-known guys at the same time. Britain's Princes Charles, William and Harry were enjoying a ski vacation, apparently unconcerned about what they might inhale in the gondolas while going up the mountain. They also seemed oblivious to the threat that trees have posed to celebrity skiers in recent times.

One would almost have to be in Prince Charles's income bracket to spend much time in Whistler. A pizza that was supposed to be large but looked more like a medium, with three soft drinks, was $40. Our one-night hotel bill looked more like a monthly mortgage payment. I guess I shouldn't complain, though, because it probably would have cost more if the room had come equipped with a telephone and a working television.

I wasn't there for the smoke or the princes. My son, Brad, the one who can inhale a $40 pizza and then ask for seconds, was playing in a hockey tournament. Brad is six foot two and weighs about 195 pounds. You can imagine how much it cost his mother and me in groceries, clothes and hockey equipment to build a son that size. His skates alone cost more than our first car.

In a momentary lapse of sanity, I agreed to be the assistant coach of the hockey team. I've asked myself numerous times why I agreed to coach a bunch of fourteen- and fifteen-year-olds. I've narrowed it down to three plausible reasons: something I ate caused me to have a momentary brain fart; I had forgotten just how bad sixteen sweaty teenagers in a confined room could smell; or I hadn't reached the required adult dosage of being told to do something unspeakable by people one-third my age.

The Whistler tournament was the finale of a very long season. In a sixteen-team league, we finished fifteenth. Between the regular season and the playoffs, we lost twenty-eight times, often by scores such as 15–0, 9–1 and 8–2. We won six games. Before the end of the regular season, our goalie quit.

However, something unusual happened in Whistler. We won two out of three games and outscored our opposition fifteen to nine. Perhaps it was the thin, high-altitude air. Maybe the boys thought the three princes were in the crowd watching them. Most likely our victories were the result of secondhand smoke inhaled by the other teams. Either way our players were amazed, and the other coaches and I were even more amazed. Winning brought out a new side to several of the players. Apparently a fourteen- or fifteen-year-old is much less likely to tell his coach to do something unspeakable when he's winning. Most amazed of all were the players' parents, who had long ago resigned themselves to watching their sons go out and lose one for the Gipper.

Hockey parents are a unique lot. Most of them come out to the games and cheer their sons, and sometimes daughters, on to victory or defeat. Some, however, don't accept their offspring's losses gracefully. The mother of a boy from a team representing a very upper-class community assaulted a referee in the parking lot of the Whistler arena. Evidently she had a few differences of opinion with him. He didn't think he was a blind, brain-dead, lower life-form, and she did.

All in all, though, it was a fun weekend. The boys were happy to be winners finally, the weather was fantastic, the scenery was beautiful and we actually did get a chance to be close to royalty. On our way back to the hotel from a game, we passed a limousine taking one of the princes to the heliport.

In a way, we had a lot in common. In the back of the limousine was a kid who was stinking rich. The kid in the back of my van was a hockey player who hadn't showered yet, and he was just stinking.

Much Ado About Stuff

It used to be that a man's home was his castle. If anything, today it's his hassle. The reason for this change comes down to one word: *stuff*. We have too much stuff to deal with. There's stuff we have to do; stuff we don't want to do; stuff that needs fixing; stuff with no instructions; stuff that keeps flashing 12:00, 12:00, 12:00 because no one can understand the instructions; stuff that doesn't grow where you want it to; stuff that grows where you don't want it to; stuff; stuff; and more stuff.

All this stuff has invaded our homes. Trying to get it together can be a hapless exercise in futility. At least it is in my house. If I was ever able to get my stuff together, I'd forget where I put most of it before I could finish.

My desk is, always has been and no doubt always will be a prize example. It's covered in stuff. I know where most of it is, though, because I use the jelly-doughnut method of organization. That doesn't mean the good stuff is hidden inside piles of other stuff. It simply means knowing what stuff is under last Tuesday's leftover strawberry-filled doughnut as opposed to what stuff I piled on top of it. It's sort of a simplified form of carbon-dating. You have to do this, because if you don't replace the doughnut fairly often, it will start growing its own stuff.

I've tried numerous measures to get my desk more organized. I've bought computer-disk file boxes, paper-clip holders, tape dispensers, pen holders, file organizers, in and out baskets and a memo-pad holder. As a result, I no longer have any usable space left on my desk, because it's covered with desk organizers. They, in turn, are covered with all kinds of stuff.

It seems this overabundance of stuff is fostered in the school system. Whenever I ask my sons what they did in school, they reply, "Stuff." If I continue along this line of questioning, I eventually get a longer, more detailed answer: "School stuff."

I think my sons are doing fairly well in Stuff 101. They both have a number of stuff projects under way, including stuff on their floors; stuff in their closets; stuff they leave all over the family room; and science stuff growing on the dirty dishes under their beds.

It's a heavy course load. Whenever I need them to do something around the house, I hear, "Well, gee, Dad, I really can't because, you know, I, like, have lots of stuff to do."

The vitally important stuff they have to do might seem trivial to an adult with no understanding of what life is all about these days. It's difficult for adults to realize they need to see that rerun of *The Simpsons* for the fifth time just to make sure they didn't miss any of the intellectual nuances.

It's only logical that this is vastly more important stuff than household chores. When I remind my offspring that they've agreed to carry out certain basic functions around the house in return for food, shelter, clothing and hockey registration, I discover, once again, that I'm in error. These mundane activities must be carefully timed to coordinate with their busy schedule, as they love to tell me.

"Could you please take out the garbage?" I ask.

"You can't just spring this on me, Dad," one son explains. "Give me some warning when you want this done.

I might have been able to fit you in, but right now I have stuff to do."

"I asked you three hours ago, two hours ago and one hour ago. We've already been through the stop-nagging discussion, and besides, right now the garbage truck is three doors down the street."

"It's your own fault, you know. You have to understand that I have more important things to do than this kind of stuff."

Despite my advancing years, I've started to catch on. Sure, it's taken me a while to realize how important it is in the fast-paced nineties to prioritize and schedule the requests for assistance. Still, my sons don't seem to appreciate my newfound enlightenment.

"Dad, I need a ride to (insert the vitally important destination of choice)."

"Well, you can't just spring this on me, son. I have stuff to do."

My Son, the World Traveler

spoke to Mike, my oldest son, recently. That might not seem to be a big deal, but in doing so, I managed to wake him from a dead sleep—in Budapest, Hungary. Knowing that my call woke him up in the middle of the night gave me almost as much enjoyment as learning that he was still alive. It felt like a small payback for all the times he awakened his mother and me when he hit the kitchen for a middle-of-the-night meal.

When Mike came home with news of a school trip to Europe, Diane and I readily gave our permission for him to go. We told him it would be a great experience, and how we wished we could have done the same thing when we were his age. He was somewhat taken aback by our enthusiasm, even when the cost of the trip came up.

"No problem," I said when he told us it would cost $2,300 plus spending money.

He could scarcely believe his ears. He had to be wondering if aliens had kidnapped his real parents and replaced them with look-alikes. We couldn't possibly be the same parents who choked at the thought of spending $170 on a pair of running shoes. He had just told us he wanted to go on a trip that would end up costing more than $3,000 and we were scarcely batting an eyelash. We let him enjoy this state of amazement for a few minutes before we let the other shoe drop.

"With all the money you're making at your part-time job, you'll have that much saved in no time," I told him.

His face fell, he stammered a bit, then he finally managed to say, "You mean you're telling me on one hand I can go to Europe, but on the other hand, you're saying I have to pay for it myself?"

"It'll be a great experience for you to save the money yourself and then tour Europe unencumbered by parents," I said. "You'll love it, and you'll look back on this and be glad you did it all yourself. It'll be something you can really be proud of accomplishing."

He gave us one of those patented teenage looks that indicated he would be satisfied with the pride of touring Europe, even if we forced him to take the money to pay for it.

During the next few weeks, we heard several stories about other kids whose parents were picking up the whole tab for the European trip. He didn't know anyone whose parents were such cheapskates.

"Aren't you lucky," I said after each of these stories was told. "You have parents who want you to get the most out of this experience by paying for it yourself."

He never seemed convinced that the luck he had was good. Eventually, however, the desire to go to Europe overcame the hope we would pay for the trip. Each payday he tucked away most of his earnings and managed to save enough to have a fairly healthy amount of spending money to take with him.

He started out in Vienna, then traveled to Budapest, where he was when we called him. Prague and Munich are still on his itinerary.

I'm really quite proud of the hardship this tour represents for my unilingual son. He's inherited my ability with foreign languages. Like me, he barely managed to squeak through compulsory French lessons, and he avoided the idea of studying any other language. His knowledge of Hungarian, Czech and German is limited to what he's picked up watching old war movies on television and visiting delicatessens. At least he won't starve, as long as he can remember words such as *strudel*, *schnitzel* and *bratwurst*.

It's been awfully quiet around the house since he left. For one thing, I haven't been awakened by his late-night kitchen assaults, and I'm not sure I can tolerate getting as much sleep as I have lately. There haven't been any of the customary daily arguments with his brother, Brad, over guardianship of the television remote control. I haven't once had to drop whatever I was doing to drive him someplace. There have been no discussions about whether or not it's his turn to set the table or wash the dishes. The walls haven't been vibrating from the sounds of CDs or computer games rumbling through his speaker system at full bass. Our grocery bill is a shadow of its former self.

I think I miss him.

I May Not Be Handy,
but I've Got
All My Fingers

Getting Down and Dirty, Richer and Poorer

One spring I paid a man $131.67 for something that would have gotten me into big trouble if I'd brought it home when I was a kid. I bought dirt—half a dump truck full. My mother would have gotten out her wooden, attitude-adjusting spoon if I'd come home with half a sneaker full. To think that her son might one day hand over a check for $131.67 for a bunch of dirt . . . well, I'm just glad she's not here to see the day.

So what possessed me to part with so much filthy lucre for so much filthy dirt?

It was my wife's idea.

Wives have the ability to come up with a logical reason for just about anything. We men just say, "Oh, uh, okay," and go back to the hockey game, forgetting about the whole thing until the next what-the-heck-is-that-in-the-driveway event.

Wives can be downright mean when they want to get their own way about these sorts of things. They'll resort to evil, conniving trickery. They'll come into the room on a Saturday morning wearing some sexy little thing and, using their sultriest tone, say something like "Honey"—deep breath, followed by a long sigh—"I'd like to get really down and dirty this weekend."

When our minds recover from the sudden oversupply of testosterone-induced excitement and capture the real meaning of what they've just said, they're already hanging up the phone after talking to the landscape-supply dealer.

There really ought to be a law.

It's always weeks later that I slap myself in the forehead when I come up with what would have been the perfect, no-cost response. Instead of "Oh, uh, okay," I should have said: "I bet if we look under the grass we'll find all kinds of dirt just sitting there."

Of course, it wasn't just any old dirt we bought. The salesman told us it was "a scientific mixture, especially formulated to ensure lasting, healthy growth." I think I've read the same thing on a granola box and, from my past experience with granola, the dirt probably tastes about the same.

Despite the marketing claims, it still looked like plain old everyday dirt to me. It was a big pile of soil, sand and steer stools. Worse, it was usurping my van's place in the driveway.

The soil came out of the dump truck in a pile that looked remarkably like the mountain in the movie *Close Encounters of the Third Kind*. I was hoping it wouldn't attract aliens. I was in too bad a mood to be hospitable to extraterrestrials. That is, unless they came in peace, with phasers locked on "shovel."

My friend Paul phoned me a couple of days after my designer dirt hit the pavement. "I think I'm getting old," he said.

He likes to tell me that because he's five or six years younger than I am, which puts him in a different age group, sometimes even two, on product registration cards. He sounded serious this time, though, like a man who had just come face-to-face with his first gray chest hair.

When I asked him what had brought on that week's

vision of impending membership in the geriatric union, he told me he was worried about getting the best shit he could. I suggested he try more fiber in his diet, and perhaps an over-the-counter laxative.

"That's not the kind of shit I mean," he said. "I'm trying to decide whether to get it from a horse or cow. It's for my lawn and garden. Only old people worry about things like that."

It was clear what had happened. Paul was getting married in a few months and planned to hold the wedding reception in his backyard. Because he had no experience with the consequences of saying "Oh, uh, okay," Heather, his fiancée, had convinced him that his lawn wasn't rich enough to be a proper backdrop for the wedding pictures.

He ended up spending the weekend covering his lawn, flower beds and a good percentage of his body with horse by-products.

Eventually our driveways became usable again, our wives were happy, our lawns were richer, we were poorer and, more important, the smell went away. Aliens never did arrive to see my mountain. We didn't see any looking over Paul's pile, either.

Although, come to think of it, some of the wedding guests . . .

The Night Godzilla Attacked the Garbageman

I'm so ashamed.

Recently my garbage didn't meet with the approval of our sanitary-solid-waste-disposal engineer and his personal driver. I had cut up the cereal boxes, squashed the egg cartons, double-bagged the kitty litter, affixed the proper identifying stickers and provided the certified results of our family's most recent blood tests. But apparently I had neglected to cut and squash two of the tin cans properly, so he left it all behind.

When I was a child, garbagemen, as they were called then, walked up the driveway, carried your cans to the truck and returned them empty, no matter what condition your soup tins were in. All of this was accomplished at about 4:00 a.m., so that you could pick the lids out of the rose-bushes on your way to work. If they didn't like the way you packaged last Thursday's tuna surprise, they could retaliate by drop-kicking the can into your garage door.

I recall waking up several times in the night to the sound of my father running to battle stations on his "ship," screaming "Mayday! Mayday!" after hearing a direct hit on the starboard garage door. In his subconscious, the noise must have sounded like a German Fokker crashing into the poop deck. Unfortunately, taking that route through our house meant he would plunge overboard at the top of the stairs, even though he was still less than halfway to the lifeboat station.

Raccoons were the other garbage problem in our neighborhood. When they tipped over the garbage cans in the middle of the night, they often sent Dad running for a lifeboat. Sitting alone, bruised and battered on the bottom step one night, he decided to retaliate against the little beasts.

When he wasn't charging after imaginary Nazi planes and gunboats, my father was a photographer—not professionally, just annoyingly. He belonged to several camera clubs and spent his time trying to take pictures that might win contests. If I close my eyes, I can still see the outline of flashbulbs.

In the mid-fifties, flashbulbs were huge things filled with coils of magnesium, all the better to blind an unsuspecting four-year-old whose father tried to get the perfect picture of his son waking up in the morning. Our poor old dog went blind, but at least we have several hundred pictures of her. But Dad's hobby gave him the answer to the raccoon problem.

He put a trip switch in the lid of the garbage can and connected it to a camera which, in turn, was wired to set off a barrage of flashbulbs. He was rewarded on the very first night. As he sat there at the bottom of the steps wondering why the lifeboat station had been wallpapered, he remembered where he was, and that he had booby-trapped the garbage can. So he limped to the driveway and retrieved the camera.

It was clear he had scared the raccoons, because the trellis was toppled and the roses trampled. Looking at the damage to the bushes, he pictured an entire herd of garbage-eating, sleep-disturbing raccoons fleeing the scene.

Several of them must have tried to climb the trellis at once; after all, it was heavy, anchored in concrete and fastened to the wall, all the way to the top of the second story.

Since Dad was wide awake, anyway, he took the film directly to his darkroom and developed a spectacular wildlife picture of the rarely seen *sanitarus timidius*, aka the wide-eyed, slack-jawed, empty-bladdered garbageman.

I can imagine what went through the poor man's mind. It must have seemed like the bright white light people report seeing during a near-death experience. Since fire-breathing resurrected dinosaurs were big box-office hits back then, he might have felt the need to climb the trellis to escape from the one that had just lit up the night. Whether it was God or Godzilla, he didn't want to stick around to find out.

It was several weeks before garbage was picked up at our house again. When collection resumed, it became a weekly ritual for the can to hit the garage door, and for Dad to wake up at the bottom of the stairs. Eventually, sometime around 1956, he stopped worrying about the Fokkers and we all slept much better.

Dad died in 1983, but after my garbage was rejected, I think I heard his voice telling me what I should do about it. I can't wait until the pictures get back from the photofinisher.

Please Do Not Disturb—
I'm Already Disturbed Enough

It happened again the other night. It's almost become a ritual. Just as we were in the final throes of throwing our dinner together, in hopes of eating it while it was still above room temperature, the telephone rang.

"Hello, may I speak with Mr. or Mrs. Kirkland?" asked the young voice on the other end.

Sometimes the voice on the line speaks understandable English, but always in the monotone of a Grade 3 student reading aloud.

Many of you might find the nerve to tell such intruders to go forth and do whatever you might want to tell them to do with themselves. Hearing a Grade 3 monotone on the phone asking to speak with either my wife or me, I once did precisely that. It taught me the importance of identifying callers before telling them to go forth and do whatever I might want to tell them to do with themselves.

"Don't you idiots wear watches?" I screamed into the phone, although I might have used some choicer nouns and adjectives. "This is the time most people choose to eat their dinner. I have no desire to hear about your vacuum cleaners, furnace cleaning or charity for children deprived of eating anything that resembles the stuff that's growing steadily cold on my plate."

Unfortunately I later learned the caller was my son's teacher—my son's Roman Catholic school teacher. She sounded like a third-grader reading aloud because she had spent the entire afternoon listening to third-graders—including mine, who had used an inappropriate word when he lost his place on the page. I told her I had no idea where he could have learned a word like that. I doubt if she believed me, though, as the word spoken aloud in class sounded similar to one of the many I had injected into the poor woman's ear.

As a result of that incident, I now wait to hear the start of spiels before I make any suggestions about how the callers might better spend their time. I'm getting pretty good at it, because I get so much freaking practice. In days gone by, I've been called by people wanting to sell me:

- The newspaper that is already being delivered to the puddle closest to my front door
- A vacuum cleaner (ours still sucks)
- Children's books, such as *Yertle the Turtle*, which is indelibly imprinted in my mind because of the 18,304 times I had to read it in the early eighties when my sons were in that phase
- A compact disc to bring back memories of the forties (I was born in 1953)
- A time-share skiing vacation (I'm a paraplegic)
- Another vacuum cleaner
- A cheaper long-distance service
- Life insurance, although the caller declined my offer to buy a policy on his life with me as the beneficiary
- Tickets to a magic show (I asked if they could make telephone solicitors disappear)
- Yet another vacuum cleaner

Running my business from home means a number of other distractions, most of which want money. In my time, I've had work interrupted by:

- A man who just happened to have a crew in the neighborhood resealing driveways (in a snowstorm?)
- Two geriatric Jehovah's Witnesses wanting me to buy into their version of heaven
- Three different kids selling raffle tickets for the same hockey team
- My son, Mike, trying to extort money to be quiet while I wrote
- A high school student wanting pop bottles or a donation to "y'know, like, pay for my class trip to Europe"
- Two young Mormons wanting me to buy into their version of heaven
- My son, Brad, desperately needing to use my computer for his homework, which apparently involved visiting the naked supermodel Web site

As long as there are furnace ducts to clean, unsold vacuum cleaners to buy and driveways to seal, we'll all be plagued by dinnertime phone calls and unwanted knocks on the door. I suppose we should understand that these people are just trying to earn a living—or annoy enough people to gain admission to their version of heaven. Before we tell them to do whatever we might want to tell them to do with themselves, and how often, we should stop and ask ourselves one simple question: "Does that voice sound like one of the kids' teachers?"

Just Call Me
Mr. Crime Prevention

Because good neighbors warn one another when prowlers or burglars are around, one of mine came rushing over to tell me her car had been stolen—six weeks earlier. I guess she was unable to tell me sooner because she needed her car to drive the fifty feet to my place.

Her car was found on a mountain road east of town with more than $5,000 damage done to it. Since our cars are similar, she thought she should warn me. It would appear that another reason for her delay to share this information was that she wanted to tell me how much damage the thieves working in the neighborhood could inflict on cars like ours. She seemed quite proud she owned a vehicle that was so costly to repair.

It turns out that cars like ours—mine is a Plymouth Voyageur minivan—are the hot vehicles of choice for discriminating car thieves these days. Corvettes, Mercedes and BMWs have become passé for joyrides. We bought our van because of the room it gives us to transport bulky cargo such as hockey equipment, camping gear and six-foot teenage boys. The thieves are also impressed by the cargo space.

They steal the car at one stop and use it to carry the proceeds from their midnight shopping trips at computer and stereo shops.

My neighbor's van had an advantage over mine, at least in the eyes of the thieves, because it had a trailer hitch. It was perfect for them to use at their first stop down the street, where they laid claim to a boat trailer that, coincidentally, came equipped with a $35,000 boat and motor.

The time had clearly arrived when I would have to do more than just lock my car doors.

I thought about getting a car alarm, but my experience with them hasn't really filled me with confidence. A guy down the road had an expensive car-alarm system installed in his vehicle. He was prone to bragging, both about the cost of the alarm and about his need for it because his car was a classic. Somehow putting the words *classic* and *Ford Pinto* in the same phrase always seemed like an oxymoron to me.

One night a cat jumped onto the hood of his car and set off the alarm. I must admit it really was an impressive alarm. The car's lights flashed off and on. Its horn blew unceasingly. A siren wailed, and a recording of the owner's voice repeatedly boomed through a loudspeaker under the hood, a statement that can't be repeated, or even translated into language remotely repeatable. Only one resident on the street was able to sleep through the racket the alarm made. I think a few of the residents of the cemetery down the road were also startled. I just bet you can guess who the sleeping beauty was.

I still see the cat wandering around the neighborhood from time to time. It's had a dazed look and a peculiar little facial tic ever since.

One thought I had was to go to the pet shop and buy a car-guarding animal. Something like a python, or perhaps a tarantula, would surely be a great deterrent to car thieves. I changed my mind when I remembered that I'm not particularly fond of snakes and that my wife is terrified of spiders.

I nearly bought a Saudi Arabian spiny-tailed desert lizard. The only way to get one of these critters to release its hold on whatever body part it grabs is to cut off its head. But then I thought it probably wouldn't be able to distinguish me from a car thief.

I even briefly toyed with a carefully hidden squirrel trap camouflaged as the gas pedal. The scars are healing nicely, thank you.

I finally decided I'd buy one of those bars that lock onto the steering wheel so it can't be turned. The bar looks like the weapon of choice for people who want to take out the kneecaps of figure-skating opponents. So now, every time I park the car, I get in a little weight lifting while I try to fit the bar onto the steering wheel and hold it in place with two hands as I insert and turn the key with my teeth.

I'd still like to find some use for the Saudi Arabian spiny-tailed desert lizard. Perhaps it could help teenagers break some of those habits that drive parents crazy. Raid the refrigerator and find Mr. Lizard in the meat drawer. Leave your dirty laundry lying around and find Mr. Lizard in your sweat socks. Forget to flush the toilet and . . . ooh, that would really hurt.

So That's What They Mean by "House Training"

New housing developments are springing up all around my area as the city spreads its tentacles farther and farther out into the countryside. Signs pointing the way to developments with names such as Morningside Estates, Riverwynde and Ravenswood Terrace line the edge of the highway. If there was truth in advertising, these developments would be called Beside the Tracks, Below the Flood Line and Former Swamp. Somehow those names just don't have the same magical ring, though.

Each weekend carloads of happy couples are lured to sales offices by brightly colored, high-flying helium balloons. They never imagine that, just two years and several hundred dump truck loads of sand and rocks ago, tadpoles were swimming where their new dream homes are taking shape.

At the rate Sold signs are appearing, it's obvious the eager buyers are forgetting to look at the whole picture. They see the advantages of buying houses that are just a few short steps from the commuter rail station. They see themselves being whisked away each morning to their jobs in the city. They'll work downtown all day and then ride the train back home, having barely made enough to cover the high-ratio mortgage that sounds so affordable when the real estate agent says it. They're intoxicated by visions of back-yard barbecues, multiple bathrooms and gas fireplaces dancing in their heads.

It won't be until sometime after they move in that they'll suddenly realize their dream houses are also those same few short steps away from the rail line that carries cars labeled Danger, Explosives and Poison. They'll lie awake long after 4:00 a.m. with the thought burning deep into their souls that one little flaw in a track could deposit a Saskatchewan Wheat Pool rail car into the middle of their gourmet kitchens.

Diane and I shake our heads and wonder who would be foolish enough to buy one of these houses. We were certainly much more intelligent when it came to purchasing our first house. We knew exactly what we wanted and we didn't rest until we found it.

Of course, there was also that little problem of what we could afford at the time. Our budget was somewhere between "very little" and "not much." Surprisingly we found a house that fitted the bill perfectly. It had stood the test of more than seventy-five years, came with nearly three acres surrounded by hundreds more that were being used as a turf farm and had an asking price of almost exactly "not much."

Oh, sure, it had its drawbacks, but nothing as serious as a rail line waiting to hurl a flaming tanker of methane at the front window. Okay, it was forty miles outside the city, and the last five were on a dirt road. A little thing like that wasn't going to deter us, even though we didn't own a car at the time. We found a used car at a price that ate up the remainder of the difference between our "very little" and "not much."

Some advertising might have described the house as "a fixer-upper" or "a handyman's special." That didn't deter us, either. I was confident I could recognize at least four out of ten power tools in the Sears catalogue, and I thought I could figure out how to use one or two. My father had always been handy with tools and, while I had never shown anything approaching an aptitude for carpentry, plumbing or electrical work, I assumed it was an inherited skill and would come naturally.

Casting our fate to the wind was easy in that house. The wind obliged us by blowing through the window and door frames at every opportunity. At our age, we were smart enough to ask the real estate agent about the insulation in the house. Unfortunately we hadn't learned to take the assurances of a glad-handing real estate agent with a grain of salt. With the amount we spent heating the house that first winter, you'd think the government of Saudi Arabia could have taken a moment or two and sent us a thank-you note.

The new houses down the road are advertised as selling for not much more than $200,000. That's roughly $200,000 more than we paid for that first house of ours. Okay, so the river that was three-quarters of a mile away when we bought the place flowed through the basement each spring. Not once, however, did we lie awake fearing a flying, flaming rail car.

That peace of mind has to be worth at least a quarter million.

They Don't Call Me Gord "The Toolman" Kirkland for Good Reason

'll admit I'm not handy. I only own one tool that can be used for building or repairing things. It's a telephone. I use it to call people who are handy.

This was a major disappointment to my father. He was handy. Our basement was one big workshop. There were all sorts of huge pieces of equipment that seemed perfectly capable of removing what I considered necessary parts of my body. I believed that the farther I stayed away from lathes and table saws, the better my chances were to grow up intact.

One tool that stands out in my memory was something called a radial-arm saw. Just its name made me think about its amputation capability. My mother called it "your father's radio-alarm saw" because every time he turned it on her radio produced an alarmingly loud buzz.

My lack of handyman capabilities became abundantly clear when a sale flyer arrived from one of those giant hardware stores on steroids that have cropped up all over the place. I had no idea what most of the products listed could be used for, and for that I can be a little thankful, because they all seemed to have prices like $258.98. I guess that's a good price for a ten-inch compound-power miter saw, because the store put exclamation marks after the amount. If I ever need one of my miters cut, I'm sure I can find some-one who knows what a miter is, and why I may need mine cut, by picking up my trusty eight-inch telephone receiver.

There were at least a dozen different sanders listed in the flyer. Okay, I can understand the need for sanding some-thing you want to smooth or remove paint from, but I can't see the need for so many different kinds. For example, can anyone honestly say they can use a random-orbit sander? It sounds like the sort of thing that would only be useful on the Mir Space Station if a supply ship crashed into it, and how often does that happen?

Some of the tools were just plain silly. For only $308, you could buy a ten-thousand-revolution-per-minute heavy-duty plate-joiner kit with a 6.5-amp motor and a carrying case. Who would use that? If a plate breaks around my house, we throw it out. I had no idea there was a power tool for putting plates back together. It strikes me, though, that something spinning at ten thousand revolutions per minute could do a lot more damage to a piece of already broken china.

We have a lot of trouble at my house with backed-up toilets. It shouldn't surprise me that, considering the amount of food our two teenage sons, Mike and Brad, put into their bodies, they'd be able to plug a toilet with their, well, um, you know what I mean.

Mike seems to believe that a plumber fairy comes along and takes care of a blocked toilet if he leaves it alone long enough. Little does he know that his mother and I are actually the real plumber fairies, and we might decide to leave something under his pillow if he persists in his habit.

We've been using an ordinary plunger, but I now know there's a power tool that could take on the job. For just

$299, we could get something called a three-and-one-quarter-horsepower plunge router that comes with a fifteen-amp motor, an edge guide and a micro-bit depth adjustment. Sounds like the very thing I need.

But who in his right mind would buy something called a reciprocating saw? That sounds like my worst power-tool nightmare come true. I imagine every time it's used to cut a piece of wood it reciprocates by cutting into a piece of the person holding on to it. With my degree of handyman skills, it wouldn't be long before I'd have to start typing with my tongue.

Ah, the Sweet Smell of— Oh, Good Lord, What the Heck Is That?

One late April day the temperature returned to something that allowed us to keep a few windows open to let in a breath of fresh air, the sounds of birds and the smell of flowers blooming in the garden. But the smell wasn't like any blooming flower I would knowingly put into my garden. It smelled like, well, um, exactly what it was. The local farmers were spreading that certain, over-abundant, aromatic animal by-product on their fields again.

It was so bad at dinnertime that I made both of my sons check their shoes. I was convinced they had stepped in a pile of some animal's by-product. I pictured myself spending the evening rubbing carpet cleaner into foul-smelling footprints. I even considered rubbing their noses into it, because that was what we did if Nipper deposited some of her by-product on the carpet when she was a puppy. If the dumbest dog ever to get lost on a single flight of stairs learned not to put by-product on the carpet, I figured it wouldn't take too many nose rubs to teach teenage boys the same thing.

The boys were vindicated, however. Both seemed pretty relieved when they checked their shoes, because they seemed to know what I was thinking of doing to whatever culprit had erased the smell of dinner with the stench of animal by-product. They didn't have too long to gloat, though, because their mother reminded them of the house rule to remove their shoes at the front door. Since I had accused them of a far greater crime, we let them off with a suspended sentence for that infraction.

The closest farm to our house is nearly half a mile away. Everyone living between our house and his were probably checking to see if someone had tracked animal by-product onto their carpets. I was thankful I didn't live any closer. If I had, I'd probably be praying for sinus congestion.

Don't get me wrong. I'm not one of those people who move into a rural area and think farmers should start spreading unscented manure. I realize fields need to be fertilized if I want to have food on my table that I don't have to pick, milk or kill on my own.

I grew up in a rural area. Whenever we'd complain about the smell coming from our neighbors' fields, my father would say, "To a farmer, that's the smell of money." Until I fully realized what my father meant, I was afraid to stand behind a farmer in a store checkout line. If that was what his money smelled like, I didn't want to be around when he pulled out his wallet.

Some farmers get creative with their excess animal by-product. I often drive by a farm in Washington State that has a pile of the stuff a hundred feet in diameter and twenty-five feet deep. Over the years, it's composted into a sizable hill of rich soil. If you want to know where the grass is greener, it's there. Some people might take that soil and put it in their flower beds, or sell it to city folks so they could do the same. Not this farmer. He saw that hill as a chance to express his patriotic pride. I can only imagine the conversation he had with his wife when he came up with the idea.

"Say, honey, you know that big old pile of bull by-product we got out back? Well, I think it'd be a right nice patriotic thing to do if we put a miniature Statue of Liberty on top of it."

She must have agreed. Sitting there on top of that old manure pile is an honest-to-goodness likeness of the big lady from the New York harbor. The farmer has even run an electrical line out to her so that the lamp in her raised hand can cast an eerie glow across the manure pile at night. The thing is about fifteen feet tall. Last year he added a huge flagpole, with an equally huge flag flapping from it. Beneath the flagpole is a light display that spells out "Old Glory" in Christmas lights.

I think the health authorities should send a picture of that display to every farmer in North America, with a warning that says: "Inhaling too much animal by-product could cause you to do something like this."

I wonder how long I can hold my breath.

Society Is
a Box of Chocolates
with Too Many Nuts

Justice Is Blind— and Her Dog Just Peed in My Cornflakes

Opportunity came knocking one day, but before I got to the door it left. Just my luck. When opportunity finally knocked, it wanted to play nicky-nicky-nine-doors.

I fully expected to be showered with wealth, fame, book contracts, television interviews and the whole bit. Benefits like that seemed certain after the envelope arrived in the mail. It wasn't some paltry thing, like being invited to be a five-time winner on a rigged game show. No one had discovered a secret will naming me as the sole heir to the trivial Howard Hughes estate. It was even better than having Dick Clark and Ed McMahon offer to bring me a check for $10 million.

I got a summons for jury duty!

The excitement of the idea built as my appointment with destiny grew closer. I spent countless hours wondering what kind of juror I should be. There have been so many examples of differing juror styles lately. I wanted to carefully select the best one to emulate.

Should I be a lone holdout for a decision—the opposite of the other jurors, as in the movie *12 Angry Men*? Even if the evidence was clear, I could play the devil's advocate. I'd force all the other jurors to endure living in a classy hotel with cable TV, room service and a health club until they all decided to agree with me. It could take months of massages, hot tubs and adult movies. Then, once I'd swung them all over, I'd change my mind and agree with their first verdict.

Perhaps I could be like the jurors who left everyone on the planet shaking their heads and asking, "What do you mean he's not guilty?"

After retiring to the jury room to ponder our verdict, I could say, "Look, folks, you know he's guilty. I know he's guilty. But to find him guilty we'll have to sit in this room for the next week. It's Friday afternoon. Let's call for a few beers, deliberate on who had the sleaziest lawyer, go back into court in a couple of hours and say we found him not guilty. There are people out in the hall who want to give us book contracts and invitations from Jay Leno and David Letterman, and we'll still get home in time to watch ourselves on the eleven o'clock news."

It would pass on the first ballot.

I could be a hard-nosed, letter-of-the-law sort of juror. I'd try to persuade my fellow jurors to impose the death penalty, even if it was only for jaywalking. Most jaywalking offenses are premeditated, so that would make the defendant guilty with special circumstances. They could probably convince me to show a little compassion and agree to punitive damages of $34 million. (It has to be a record amount to get those book contracts and Leno invitations.)

I could cause a scandal and get kicked off the jury halfway through the trial. The grocery-store checkout newspapers would make me famous. I can imagine the headlines:

- Juror Removed for Discussing the Case with Elvis Presley
- Juror Abducted by Aliens, Taken Back in Time to Watch the Crime
- Juror Found to Be Defendant's Long Lost Love Child
- Juror Predicts World Will End Before the Trial Does
- Exclusive Pictures of Juror's Conjugal Visit with Female Prosecutor

When I finally left for court, I was still undecided about which type of juror to be. Approaching the courthouse doors, I stopped to read the plaque under the statue of an imposing man. It was Hanging Judge Bailey, the Canadian equivalent of America's famous Judge Roy Bean. I took that as a sign. There wouldn't be a jaywalker alive after I finished performing my judicial duties.

As I waited in line with my summons, I practiced my juror facial expressions—stern, serious but open-minded, shocked and uncommitted. At last I handed my papers to the clerk, who looked at them briefly before she shattered my dreams.

"We don't need you," she said. "They reached a last-minute plea bargain. We might call you back in a few years."

Two weeks' worth of fantasies evaporated in an instant. No book contract. No hotel with massages, hot tubs and adult movies. No invitation to sit in the big chair beside Leno's desk. No headlines in the grocery-store papers.

As I left the courthouse, I looked as dejected as the guys leaving divorce court. I glanced up at the statue of Hanging Judge Bailey. The expression on his face said it all.

There just ain't no justice in this world.

Is an Ordinary Cup of Coffee Too Much to Ask?

It's almost become too difficult to buy a simple cup of coffee. There are just too many indecisions to make.

I guess my tastes are fairly simple. I like my coffee hot, black and strong enough to wake me up. I don't want to think about anything before I've had a cup of coffee. Truth be known, I'm barely able to think about anything before I've had a cup of coffee. Some people, especially those in my immediate family, don't think I'm that great a thinker after my coffee, either.

I've come to the conclusion that the plain old run-of-the-mill cup of coffee should be put on the endangered-species list. An experience I had one morning would seem to prove my point.

"I'll have a black coffee, please," I asked the waitress.

Apparently we aren't supposed to call them waitresses anymore. They prefer to be called coffee barristas now.

"Regular or decaf?" she asked with a look that told me I should have known to specify.

"Regular," I said, hoping that would end the conversation and let me get some caffeine into my system before I nodded off.

"Do you want Indonesian Java, Kenyan Mountain Grown, Colombian Organic, Guatemalan Extra, Turkish Double Strength or West Seattle Rainwater?"

"Uh, I'll just have a plain black coffee, please," I begged, not wanting to overtax my thinking capabilities before adding coffee to my bloodstream.

"But what kind do you want?" the barrista pressed with a slight tinge of frustration in her voice.

"Does it really matter? I just want a cup of coffee—plain, old, hot, black coffee."

"Well," she said with a definite and unpleasant edge to her voice, "if you order Indonesian Java, you're supporting the repressive government there. Kenyan Mountain Grown might have been picked by child labor, Colombian Organic and Guatemalan Extra both support farmers wanting to break free of the powerful cocaine cartels, Turkish Double Strength supports another government with a questionable civil-rights record and West Seattle Rainwater is our house blend."

"I'll take the house blend," I said, hopeful I'd soon have a hot cup in my hands.

I should have known better.

"As a latte, cappuccino, espresso or café Americano?" she asked.

"Look, I'm not awake," I said, hoping she'd show some pity. "I just want a plain cup of coffee that doesn't take any decisions. Can you just pour some coffee into a cup and give it to me?

"Short, tall or grande?"

"Large."

"We don't have large. You have to specify short, tall or grande."

I assumed that grande would be the biggest and prayed that would be the end of it. It probably would have been, except I remembered I hadn't had breakfast before venturing out in search of caffeine.

"Could I get a Danish with that, please?" I asked.

"We don't have Danish. We have almond biscotti, chocolate biscotti or mocha biscotti," she said, pointing at some small cookies. "They're $2.95 each."

For $2.95 I wanted something that looked as if it would take more than two bites to eat, so I passed on the biscotti and handed over $3.59 for my West Seattle Rainwater grande. It looked strikingly similar to the plain old run-of-the-mill large black coffee I normally pay eighty-five cents for. The only noticeable difference was that it wasn't in a heat-resistant foam cup. In keeping with the environmental concerns of the new breed of coffee drinkers, I was holding a paper cup that transferred the heat from the coffee to the palm of my hand faster than you could say, "Holy crap! That's hot!"

By the time I reached my car, I was trying to hold the cup with as little skin contact as possible. I was afraid to look at my hand, fearing it had turned into a smoldering lump of charcoal. Trying to fumble for my car keys and maintain some control of the thermonuclear grande cup proved impossible. It came down to a subconscious decision. I either had to drop the coffee or check into an emergency ward for skin grafts. My $3.59 West Seattle Rainwater grande made a dark brown twelve-ounce puddle beside my car door.

I wasn't about to go through all that again to get another cup, so I drove around the corner to the minimart at a gas station and asked the clerk for a large black coffee.

"Colombian, Kona, Irish Cream or Hazelnut Raspberry?" he asked.

"Forget it," I said, hoping to get my caffeine in another form. "Just give me a Coke."

"Classic, diet, caffeine-free or cherry?"

Yes, Doctor, that was when I had the nervous breakdown.

My Ribs Are Togetherness-Challenged

I managed to break three of my ribs once. I tried to stand up and missed.

As I've already mentioned elsewhere, I no longer have full use of my legs. I injured my spine in a serious golfing accident in 1990. My car was rear-ended on the way to the golf course. It had a rather profound effect on my handicap.

I know, I know. I'm not supposed to use words like *handicap* anymore. Apparently the term comes from a time when disabled people earned their money by begging with their hands or caps held out. Political correctness demands we use a more discreet term for just about everything from person-hole covers to consistency-reduced peanuts, or peanut butter.

All kinds of new products have been brought about by political correctness. Many of them are developed with the best intentions but end up missing the mark. The Mattel toy company introduced a new friend for Barbie not so long ago. Share a Smile Becky is a strawberry blond (aren't they all?) who's physically disabled, mobility-challenged, physically impaired, differently abled and mobility-disenfranchised.

Personally I think Mattel is to be congratulated for the realistic portrayal of someone who's physically disabled, mobility-challenged, physically impaired, differently abled and mobility-disenfranchised. Becky's hot pink wheelchair is incredibly realistic. It's so realistic that it doesn't fit through the door of Barbie's house.

There are countless doors that my wheelchair won't fit through. Probably the most ironic is the door to the washroom for people who are physically disabled, mobility-challenged, physically impaired, differently abled and mobility-disenfranchised that isn't wide enough to allow my chair to pass.

It's amazing how many store owners don't want money from people in wheelchairs. My local outlet of that famous national chain that sells automotive services, sporting goods and household items is a perfect example. Like most of their stores, this one has a turnstile blocking the entrance. Some stores have a gate to allow wheelchairs through, but the one down the road has welded its gate shut.

I was able to get into the store on one occasion by wheeling through the automotive-repair bays. Once inside I discovered that the aisles were too narrow. Along the entire length of the first aisle, my chair punctured holes in bags of potting soil, peat moss, fertilizer and sand, creating a miniature range of mountains beneath the bags. I left before they attracted store security or real estate salespeople.

Unfortunately the forces against reality in toys have stepped in. Mattel will redesign Barbie's house so that her friend Becky can come over to play. I can assure you that none of my friends redesigned their houses after my accident. In fact, after looking into the cost involved, I didn't even redesign my own house for my wheelchair. Thankfully, for short distances, I'm able to use crutches that clip onto my arms.

It's the same altered reality that's forced Barbie to sustain a relationship with a eunuch for so many years. Had reality been allowed to prevail, that marriage wouldn't have lasted anywhere near this long, because Ken is nether-region-challenged. Mattel could have introduced a line called Divorced Barbie, the doll that comes with all of Ken's accessories.

I can't wait for Becky's accessories to appear. Because she's physically disabled, mobility-challenged, physically impaired, differently abled and mobility-disenfranchised, she'll need Becky's Neurology Ward. She can call on Dr. Barbie to perform the same test I had recently. Remember applying electrodes to dead frogs in science class to make their nerves twitch? I played the frog.

Dr. Barbie can prescribe the same painkiller I took that night. It didn't do anything for the pain, but it altered my thinking so that I didn't care if it hurt. It altered my thought processes, too. I thought I could stand up without the crutches.

If Becky does that, she'll probably break three ribs, as well—or should I say three of her ribs will be togetherness-challenged, wholeness-disenfranchised, dimensionally altered . . .

Whatever Happened to Plain Old Everyday Crayons?

It happens every year. Just in time for Christmas a major toymaker announces a radical change in its product line. Any child who owns the previous version will be rendered hopelessly out of date.

Anyone with children fears the words *new and improved*. They're fine when it comes to laundry detergent, but when used in any connotation involving toys, they really mean "eneless $econd ver$ion to $tick it to parent$."

Nintendo begot Super Nintendo which, in turn, begot Nintendo 64. Gameboy begot Virtual Boy. Sega begot Sega CD which, in turn, begot Sega Saturn. I doubt these companies instill planned parenthood into their products, and all this begetting will continue.

The results of our own begetting can't live without the most current clone of the original. Ogre that I am, I'm willing to leave my sons without the essential necessities of life. Instead I'll frivolously fritter away my money on food, mortgage payments and clothing.

This time it's the Crayola people who have gotten into the begetting act. They've replaced their current line of scented crayons. Gone are coconut, licorice, chocolate and blueberry aromas. The company points out that it's reacting to parents' fears that kids are more likely to eat these food-scented crayons than color with them.

At least the original scents made some sense.

Baby powder, I assume, is white. Whenever I think of real baby powder, my mind immediately leaps back to the diaper change that usually necessitated using the stuff on one of my sons. Included in that memory was an entire array of aromas that filled the room whenever I used baby powder. If the Crayola people have included these smells in their baby-powder crayon, then we can be pretty sure children won't eat it. Odds are they may not even want to color with it.

What color is leather jacket? Once it could be safely assumed it would be black. Today it could be the team color of any major-league sports franchise.

What does a leather jacket smell like? If it's a new jacket, the answer is obvious. However, to have the authentic leather-jacket smell, Crayola will have to include oil, grease, exhaust fumes, beer and, in the Montreal area, exploded pipe bombs.

Dirt must be brown, but just what shade of brown is the company referring to?

I'll bet whoever made this decision is some childless person with a master of business administration. It shows the brilliance displayed by a lot of people with MBAs. The abbreviation indicates their ability to think clearly—misguidedly below average.

If Crayola is trying to prevent kids from eating its product, why make it smell like dirt? Take a look in any sandbox. Dirt is one of the mainstays of the childhood diet. If my mother dropped a recipe ingredient on the kitchen floor, she would always pick it up, throw it into the mixing bowl and proclaim, "Oh, well, you have to eat a peck of dirt before you die." That way no food was ever wasted in our house. I've eaten oatmeal dirt cookies, butter dirt tarts and even spaghetti with dirtballs.

Crayola's most obscure scent is new car. No doubt this was another MBA decision. Drive by any car lot. It would be easier to come up with the secret to the meaning of life than to pinpoint exactly what color new car is. Sure, once new cars came in any color, as long as it was black, but not today. None of them are red, blue, green, yellow, orange, brown, black or purple. What I consider to be my red-and-gray van is actually wildberry and sterling.

I asked a group of kids to tell me what color a new-car-scented crayon should be, and just what they thought a new car smelled like. I got a variety of answers.

"Our new car is blue and the dog threw up in it on the first day, so I guess the crayon should be blue and smell like dog barf."

"If you didn't have that club thing on your steering wheel, my brother's next new car would look and smell a lot like yours."

I can't wait until Crayola tries to scent the flesh-tone crayon. Aside from the fact that I have never met anyone whose complexion is that color, can you imagine the potential unappetizing smells?

How about postgame hockey dressing room?

Avoid Hassles with Canada Customs— Carry a Surface-to-Air Missile

Canadian writers who develop a taste for the finer things in life—food, clothing and shelter—eventually look at a map of North America and say, "I wonder what's in that green blob underneath the pink one."

One day I decided to see if 'Murica, the land of the free and the home of the Braves, would be a place for this Canadian writer to seek fame and fortune.

It was like joining a party after the guest list was lost. Not only was I welcomed into the great melting pot, it was even accepted that I was supposed to be there. Strange folks these 'Muricans. They were happy to see another writer join the fold. No matter how hard I looked, I couldn't find a trace of any government inquiries trying to protect American culture, bookstores or radio from the demon horde of foreign competition. They don't even realize that civilization, as they know it, will crash around them unless they start spending millions of dollars studying the impact of domestic bookstores selling foreign writers' books.

Canadians could sure teach those 'Muricans a thing or

two, but since they're so painfully unaware of the threat I pose to their nation, I'm joinin' the party!

Following a suggestion from my new agent, I established a US mailing address at a post office a couple of hundred yards south of the border in Sumas, Washington. That was when the trouble started.

On my first visit to pick up my eagerly anticipated mail, I spent the grand total of twenty-five minutes outside the country. Fifteen of those were in the lineup at the border. I told the Canada Customs officer how long I'd been away, and that I was bringing back an ad for a grocery store and the fall calendar for the local vocational/technical school. His facial expression clearly indicated he thought I was full of bovine excrement.

I was ordered to open my car. He wanted to ensure I could tell he had passed the customs-officer course, Giving Stern Looks to Law-Abiding Citizens 101. He proceeded to look into every nook and cranny in my car. He even found a couple of nooks and two or three crannies I didn't know were there. I was hoping he didn't want to examine a few of my more personal crannies.

He left no piece of paper unexamined, and believe me, my van carries enough pieces of paper to jump-start a recycling program. He even tried to dismantle my crutches to see what I had hidden inside them. He examined all of the contents of my briefcase, glove box and litter bag, which has occasionally been known to carry actual litter.

And then he found it: the small black bag I have to carry wherever I go.

When he opened it, he probably thought he had found the mother lode of customs-officer euphoria. The bag contains the medical supplies I have to use because of my paraplegia: sterile alcohol swabs, tubes of anesthetic gel, syringes, dozens of rubber gloves and some peculiar-looking plastic tubes, the use for which is best left unsaid.

He held one of the tubes aloft and demanded to know

what it was in his best rendition of the stern and forceful tone of voice they teach at the Matchbook Correspondence Customs Officer and Neurosurgery School.

So I told him.

I told him in great detail about the proper use of each and every item he found in the bag. No anatomical information was untold. I went on and on, ignoring his mumbled pleas to stop. I was feeling a bit like Arlo Guthrie in the song "Alice's Restaurant." I wished I had "forty-seven eight-by-ten color glossy photographs with circles and arrows and a paragraph on the back of each one telling what it was."

The officer was barely audible as he closed my car door and said I could leave. I drove off feeling like an unwelcome guest in my own country. He returned to his post and the difficult job of ignoring people who import handheld, surface-to-air missiles through our country so they can shoot down civilian aircraft.

The mind boggles at the thought of how hard that must be.

If Fire Can Be Harnessed, Where Do You Put the Bridle?

The owners of the first cave on the block to have a fire blazing under their baby-bison ribs were probably looked at by the neighbors the same way we once looked at our first neighbors with a television. Similarly our children describe, with youthful awe and jealousy, the people down the street who have the latest development in computer technology.

Those prehistoric ancestors could brag about being able to serve two charbroiled all-beast patties on a sesame-tree leaf. Fire let them discard the recipe for sushi and mastodon tartar. Unfortunately anthropologists dug it up again this century and thought it sounded appetizing. They were wrong.

Historians, sociologists and anthropologists all tell us that one of the most significant events in our species' history was the harnessing of fire. However, fire has ignored these learned scholars, because it doesn't seem to know it has been harnessed.

Our inability to harness fire has been clearly demonstrated in two Associated Press news items I came across. Both of them were about fire, inflatable devices and the statements of the people involved.

A story from Anchorage, Alaska, detailed the destructive power of fire . . . and pillows. Apparently Damie Thomas was overwhelmed by red flashes and a deafening boom in her bedroom. While that, in itself, might bring to mind an intriguing image of what she was doing, the story goes on to say that she was hospitalized with minor burns after attempting to inflate her air mattress with a hair dryer.

She turned on the dryer, using its lowest setting, and stuck it over the nozzle of the blue velvet double-size mattress. The ensuing explosion, which was later linked to a tire-sealing compound her husband had used to fix a leak, blew the bedroom door off its hinges, shattered the window and impaled her pillow in the ceiling. Ms. Thomas's hair, the carpet and the curtains were singed.

"It was a freak thing," she said.

Hopefully Saddam Hussein hasn't heard about this particular freak thing. If he learned that a pillow could be turned into a high-power weapon, he could unleash the mother of all pillow fights. He'd be using blue velvet air mattresses and hair dryers to launch Scud missiles armed with wall-impaling pillows.

Fire also created havoc for Mike Selivanoff, the county engineer for Garfield County, Washington. The fire, on a county road north of metropolitan Pomeroy, Washington, didn't appear to be harnessed. One had to feel sorry for government officials who, despite trying to do something good, messed up big-time. We've all had those kinds of experiences. Luckily for us, our well-intentioned blunders don't get covered by Associated Press reporters.

It all started as a recycling project. Any project that is based on the improvement of the environment is supposed to bring praise to the government officials who conceive it. On the surface, this one looked good. It was the result under the surface that caused the problem.

The county shredded a half-million discarded tires and mixed them with gravel to fill a gully in an attempt to shore up the roadbed. After the mixture was put in place, more gravel was poured on top.

Old tires create a number of solid-waste problems. Unfortunately, in Garfield County, they forgot about one of those problems, and it was the cause of their current situation.

Tires burn.

Not only that, they have a habit of spontaneously erupting. When the tire bits became saturated with groundwater, the rusting process in the steel belts was accelerated. Rusting steel can produce enough heat to ignite rubber.

And it did.

Traffic is now rerouted away from this three-hundred-foot section of the road. Not long ago, steam began escaping from the roadbed. Soon flames as high as a foot and a half started shooting out of the road surface.

Mr. Selivanoff is trying to put a positive spin on the steaming, smoking and flaming road. Perhaps it can become a tourist attraction. After all, tourists flock to let the road tow them up Magnetic Hill in New Brunswick. Why wouldn't they want to get hot wheels in Washington?

"It's kind of scenic, more than anything else, like driving through Yellowstone National Park," Selivanoff says.

Clay Barr, the county's director of emergency services, has a somewhat different opinion of the road. His comment will probably destroy the tourism potential. "It stinks," he says.

Whatever it is—freaky, scenic or stinky—I think they'd all tell you that you can't harness a fire. There's just no place to attach the bridle.

I Don't Have Multiple Personalities— and Neither Do I

As a humor columnist, I tend to look at life's events and see the incongruencies between them. Sometimes I look at occurrences within my own family. Other times I draw from the deep well of weirdness found all around us.

Recently I learned I'm "a typical West Coast liberal socialist wacko." Apparently certain people in Canada's federal Reform Party didn't like my analogy that Nipper, my cerebrally challenged cocker spaniel, is smarter than some of its Members of Parliament because she likes everyone, no matter what their race, religion, gender, sexual orientation or political affiliation is.

I guess I could ease up a bit on the Reform Party. After all, I, more than anyone, should know better than to poke fun at people with physical disabilities. I find it hard enough getting around on my crutches; I can't imagine what it would be like to try to get around with both feet lodged in my mouth.

So, in this spirit of compassion for Reform, I won't be

writing about the party's provincial candidate in British Columbia, the one who spoke about women's and aboriginal studies courses at the University of Northern British Columbia. Don't expect to hear from me that he said, "Where else can you study Indians and lesbians in such great depth?"

Not long ago, I learned from one of my editors that a reader had referred to me as "a psycho Nazi fascist." Apparently I had touched a nerve with this person in one of my columns about government spending decisions.

I'm not sure if he or she was overly sensitive when I questioned the decision by Ontario Premier Mike Harris to lay off several herds of public servants. It just didn't make sense that these jobs were expendable. When Harris's predecessor, Bob Rae, was premier, the province had to spend more than $4 million to have a private consulting firm count the government's computers because there were too many for busy civil servants to inventory.

So I guess I shouldn't be too critical of civil servants. Of course, that means I won't be writing about the brain power exhibited by the employees of BC Hydro who are responsible for Dowton Lake, north of Pemberton, in central British Columbia. You'll have to read someone else if you want to know what happened when they decided to lower the level of the lake. I'll refrain from mentioning that they forgot to stop the flow before they left, and that Dowton Lake, which used to be ringed with forest and mountains, is now Dowton Puddle, surrounded by mud and dead or dying fish and marine plants.

Or perhaps I've raised the ire of someone who came out of university with a degree in sociology or anthropology. After all, I once questioned the need for studies such as "Career Markers and Personal Performance Strategy Development of Expert and Novice Symphony Conductors and Professional Hockey Coaches," a bargain at only $105,000.

I realize I shouldn't criticize someone merely because the education they chose to get left them prepared for life in the twelfth century. In future I won't wonder who the doorknob was who approved a grant of $35,000 to write "Craft Industries in Postmedieval Iran: Ceramics, Metalwork, Glass." Of course, I'll also have to come to the conclusion that it's much more important to spend $100,670 in tax money on an interactive study of video games than on health care or education. To heck with anyone who needs open-heart surgery. We need to know more about the ecclesiastical courts in nineteenth-century England.

From now on, anything I write that might appear to be pointing out that the Reform Party is rife with bigots, or suggesting that some people might not be endowed with the brains of a root weevil, or even hinting that bureaucrats, sociologists and anthropologists are wasting the tax money we give to our governments, will just be a figment of someone else's imagination.

After all, to write a column that most of my readers say they enjoy, while at the same time being a typical West Coast liberal socialist wacko and a psycho Nazi fascist, would take someone with multiple-personality disorder, which I don't have.

And neither do I.

Time Travel Is Expensive

My family and I took a short ferry ride and ended up somewhere in 1969. The unfortunate part of this time travel was that I stayed in my forties instead of returning to my 1969 age of fifteen.

I was on a Pacific island. No, I didn't get transported to Bora Bora or one of the islands the French want to make glow in the dark. I had traveled to Saltspring Island between the British Columbia mainland and Vancouver Island. It's a refuge of aging hippies and young hippie wannabees. My sons voiced the opinion that I should feel right at home, because it's obvious I'm in the former category. They base their opinion on my musical tastes.

This island is also home to several thousand sheep. They produce the famous Saltspring Island lamb found in freezer sections across the continent. People who can bring themselves to eat lamb without feeling guilty tell me it's very good. To me, devouring lamb is somewhat akin to consuming a kitten. I'm just not someone who can eat it without feeling as if I'm one of the bad-guy coyotes from the cartoons. I expect to have a sheepdog bash me over the head with an anvil at every mouthful.

Time doesn't move slowly on this island; it came to a complete stop more than twenty-five years ago. People still earn their livings making bead necklaces and belts. Arts and craft shops and organic gardeners abound.

Capitalism seems to have made inroads, however. A half-size carving of an owl caught my eye. My wife has a thing about owls and owns an extensive collection of carvings, paintings, photographs and ceramics featuring the bird. I, being the ever-doting, wonderful husband I am, thought I'd buy this piece for her to put on the shelf that could easily be emptied if she put all my hockey books into storage. I thought the carving was a bit expensive at $49.95, but we ever-doting, wonderful husbands don't let price rule our hearts. Well, actually, we do let price rule our hearts when we find out there are no decimals on a $4,995 price tag.

I saw a man with hair down to the middle of his back, wearing a poncho that might have been washed in this decade. He was in the grocery store buying forty heads of California-grown lettuce for $1.29 a head. When we were leaving the island, he was sitting by the ferry port selling "organically grown" heads of lettuce for $3 a head. Tourists were abandoning their motor homes in the ferry lineup so they could buy his totally organic produce. Another "organic farmer" at the ferry dock was selling "local organic" sweet corn. Perhaps he hadn't noticed that in early July corn stocks are about two feet tall. His corn was as local and organic as his cohort's lettuce.

The island seems to have the highest per-capita usage of words such as *holistic, healing, crystals, organic* and *natural hemp products.* Young girls who look as if they've just returned from Woodstock—the real one, not the 1994 copycat—offer to read one's aura, colors or tarot cards.

"Like, you know, this crystal is really cool," one of these lovelies told me. "It can, like, you know, cure things like cancer and stuff. My friend, Susan, like, her grandmother, you know, used one of these to cure herself. Susan said she had something called hypochondria or something. I guess it was, like, you know, really bad. You know, you seem to be having a green day. Like, I can see it in your aura. You should, like, you know, get me to read it for you."

I might have been willing to let her read my aura, but I thought I might not understand a single, like, you know, word she said. Besides, if I was indeed having a green day, I planned on keeping it in my wallet.

People in eastern Canada often comment how laid-back people in British Columbia are, but even the most relaxed Vancouverite has difficulty slowing to the pace on the Gulf Islands. We went for a walk around the main town on the island. As we strolled past the craft shops, the T-shirt vendors and the made-in-Taiwan authentic Saltspring Island souvenir store, we came upon the local fire hall. Fire trucks stood ready to roar off to the next fire. Something was missing, however. Where were the firemen? In the door was a sign with a clock indicating they would be back in an hour. Presumably, if you happen to have a fire while they are wherever it is they will be back from, you should bring it in when they return. No doubt their motto is: "We've never lost a foundation."

I just got my Visa bill for the trip. I think my aura is having a red day.

What Was That You Just Called Me?

I'm thinking about having a pad of those peel-and-stick bits of paper permanently mounted on my chest. That way people will be able to peel one off, write the latest politically correct label they want to put on me and stick it on my forehead.

Society has always felt that people need to be labeled in some manner. Usually they focus on gender, race, religion or ethnic origin. Many of these labels were more than a little derogatory and were used to divide people into social strata. They were often found in sentences beginning with "Did you hear the one about the dumb . . ." and "Some of my best friends are . . ."

For the most part, we've turned our backs on the derogatory labels. From time to time, we still hear them and are embarrassed by the use of the term and by the user. Still, we can't get away from applying labels to just about everyone. Thus was born political correctness.

We've never been just Canadians or Americans. For some reason, people identify themselves with the country that some great-great-grandfather left in disgust in the 1800s. Those people who drive with bumper stickers that say "Kiss Me, I'm Irish" must have forgotten that old Gramps gladly left Ireland for good when the hash browns became scarce.

Politically correct labels change daily. It's enough to make one feel like an old preserve jar that keeps changing from strawberry jam to green tomato pickles and then on to prune delight. We're constantly having new labels stuck to us, and I think I'm developing an allergy to the glue.

Politically correct language has taken that relatively small list of epithets that was once used and expanded it beyond comprehension. The original concept of attempting to avoid insulting one another has reached epidemic proportions. Now we have to fear insulting someone by referring to them with what we think is a politically correct word or phrase but don't realize has been replaced and is now considered politically incorrect.

It's a little like going through customs. If you don't make the officers suspicious, you can get through with your case of assault rifles fairly easily. If one of their dogs smells a poppy-seed bagel, it will assume you have the annual heroin production of Burma in your carry-on luggage. The customs folk will be even more unpleasant than usual. They'll point guns and rectal-examination tools in your general direction. Similarly, if you use the current politically correct label for someone, you can continue your conversation with little more than a comma. If you slip up and use the one that's been suddenly replaced, the keepers of political correctness become even more anal than usual. You can expect to have withering looks and explicit adjectives aimed your way.

In a radio interview I did a while ago, the host was concerned he might have slipped up and used an antiquated adjective when he referred to my ability to move from one place to another. I'm glad that terms like *gimp* and *cripple* have fallen into disuse, but I get confused about what label to apply to myself based on how well I get from point

A to point B. Over the past few years, so many terms have come and gone that I'm constantly afraid I'll use the wrong one and offend myself. *Handicapped* and *disabled* are frowned on now. Am I *physically challenged* this week, or should I say *mobility-impaired*? Do I call myself *differently abled* or *a person with differing abilities*. Wouldn't it be easier to call me Gordon?

I'm glad my wife doesn't let me put ads in the personals section of the newspaper classifieds. The labels people use to describe themselves when advertising for Mr. or Ms. Right could become passé before the presses roll. Because of the cost, people have reduced their labels to abbreviations. Marital status, sexual preference, habits and just about every other detail of life has been reduced to a few letters.

It takes a while, but eventually you can learn to translate things like "DWSPF/NS/SD seeks DMSSGBPWM/NS for interest and mutual benefits." For the uninitiated, this is a divorced white straight professional female who is a non-smoker and a social drinker looking to meet a divorced, married or single, straight, gay or bisexual professional white male nonsmoker to purchase guaranteed investment certificates and mutual funds.

I guess that makes me a MWM/PC/MI/DA/PWDA/-NS/SD/MCP—or something.

Read This, or You'll Hear from My Lawyers

I was so proud. I thought it would take me a lot longer and a great deal more American publication credits to be accepted into the culture of the United States. After all, as a Canadian writer, I've had certain hurdles to get over down there, such as convincing people that Canadians don't have to write everything in both English and French unless we're dealing with the government.

Recently, in the mail, I got an invitation that demonstrated I was welcome in the land of opportunity, even though I continue to live north of the forty-ninth parallel. I could barely contain my excitement when I realized the document was indeed an invitation to join with others in the Great American Pastime.

No, not baseball, the other Great American Pastime.

I was invited to take part in a class-action lawsuit.

It wasn't anything spectacular, like the ones for exploding breast implants or corroding birth-control devices. My gender kept me from participating in those cases. Still, the case involved a corporation not living up to its responsibilities. I was surprised that the people who started the lawsuit were considering accepting a proposed settlement, even though it didn't include a provision for sentencing the company president to his choice of either lethal injection or electrocution.

A corporation whose product I bought apparently failed to deliver promotional rebates to some of its customers quickly enough. When I purchased a piece of computer hardware a while ago, the company was offering a small cash rebate, along with some software, as a purchase incentive. Neither the amount of money involved nor the software had anything to do with my decision to buy the product, but I sent in my coupon and proof of purchase just the same. After several weeks, the money and the software arrived, and I assumed that would be the end of it.

I forgot about the Great American Pastime down there in the Litigious States of America.

From the gist of what I was able to translate from the legalese in the document, some people felt it took the company too long to get those goodies in the mail. Since they had so much time on their hands while they waited, they decided to put together a class-action suit.

Excuse me? Let's get serious here for a moment. If we're going to start suing because a rebate took a little longer to get to us, then we should also be suing over much more important issues. I can think of several things I'd be more interested in hauling someone into court over.

When we bought our dog, Nipper, we assumed she came fully equipped with a functioning brain. Obviously the breeder was negligent in selling us a dog so stupid she can get lost on a single flight of stairs. Let's get all the people who have ever owned a cerebrally challenged canine to join forces in a class-action suit against the offending kennels.

When I was a kid, I had an incredible collection of bubble-gum cards and comic books. A lot of those cards are worth a fortune today. However, my mother threw them out when we moved after I finished Grade 8. I'd estimate my collection would be worth somewhere in the upper five figures today. Let's get together and sue every mother who ever threw out a Mickey Mantle or a Gordie Howe card in a deliberate and malicious act of housecleaning.

Even farther back there was an event that so traumatized me I hate even to bring it up. I'll bet I'm not alone. In 1958 I was fraudulently lured into joining a cult that held me captive for years. Oh, sure, they called it school to make it sound good. When my mother took me to visit something called kindergarten, I was shown a live rabbit that supposedly lived in the classroom. When I arrived the following September, there was no rabbit. It was all a sham to get me to sign up. I announced I wouldn't go if there wasn't going to be a rabbit in the room, only to be told I was stuck in a binding contract until 1972. Let's sue every teacher who ever tricked a small child into getting an education with the promise of a rabbit or other such incentive, and then failed to deliver.

I'd also like to warn Santa Claus about all this. I think this class-action-suit business might get him thinking about that new bike he promised me when I saw him at a department store in 1961. If I don't get it soon, he'll be ho-ho-ho-ing to my lawyers.

Anyone care to join me?

Feeling Fear at the Fall Fair

During the fall, fairs spring up faster than carnies can say, "Step right up and throw your money my way."

Where else can we watch Billy Joe Bob McCoy shear a sheep blindfolded, or gasp at thrilling displays of jam, pies or quilts? Who can resist the urge to buy knives that can cut through a tomato and your left index finger in a single slice? Where else can we enjoy the smell of greasy burgers, fries and hot dogs mingled with the aroma wafting from the barns and up from the puddles left behind by people who ate too many burgers, fries, hot dogs and wads of fluorescent cotton candy washed down with $2.75 colas before going for a ride on the Slingshot?

Ah, the Slingshot! This "ride" lets two fairgoers part with $85 for approximately thirty seconds of gut-wrenching excitement, provided they sign a waiver promising not to sue the fair for injury, trauma or dry-cleaning expenses. The idiots . . . I mean, thrill-seekers, are strapped into chairs that are connected to the tops of two tall towers by oversize bungee cords. At the push of a button, the lucky pair are launched 125 feet straight up. Naturally what goes up must come down, but thanks to the bungee cords, it must go back up again. After about six whiplash-inducing direction changes, the chair is lowered to the ground and the pair stagger off, wishing they hadn't eaten those burgers or drunk $13.75 worth of pop.

No fall fair would be complete without a regiment of grunting, foul-smelling, fly-attracting barnyard friends with disgusting personal hygiene. Some even brought farm animals with them; some of those were pregnant and ready to deliver during the fair.

Watching a birth isn't high on my list of exciting entertainment. Unfortunately, since Diane was preoccupied during the two occasions she was the main attraction, she wanted to watch a cow in the final stages of labor.

Oh, the thrill of it all.

Reading the signs around the stall, I noticed some similarities between the event at hand and the arrival of my own children. I quickly endeared myself with the almost totally female audience when I pointed this out.

"Cows have a nine-month gestation period just like humans," I said, trying to give Diane a feeling of oneness with the cow, which lay calmly chewing on some hay a few feet away. "And look," I added, pointing to one of the signs, "she's delivering an eighty-pound baby. After all that time you could only come up with one that was six pounds, fourteen ounces."

I thought I heard someone in the crowd murmur, "Hit him."

"The vet just said the labor would take eight hours at most," I ventured. "Eight hours to produce an eighty-pound baby. You were in labor for forty-six hours with Mike and thirty-eight with Brad. She hasn't made a sound the whole time we've been here. Not once has she looked at the bull across the aisle and said, 'You did this to me!' or 'If you ever lay another hoof on me!' The staff hasn't even called in an exorcist. Her mooing hasn't changed into a deep, satanic voice the way yours did, dear."

The murmuring grew. Clearly I was stimulating a lot of discussion among the women in the audience. Above their conversations I heard, "Why don't you try having a kid, buster?"

"I've had two," I countered. "Labor didn't bother me as much as it seemed to bother my wife, though."

I decided it might be best to leave the area about then, especially when I heard Diane join in the murmuring chorus.

"Smack him!"

"Crucify him!"

"Pull his upper lip over his head so he knows what it feels like!"

"Put him on the Slingshot without the seat belts!"

Diane found me a couple of hours later, still hiding from the mob. The calf had arrived about an hour after I left. She told me all the details about things like placenta, fluids and other birth stuff that generally leave men wanting to cover their ears and sing, "La La La, I Can't Hear You." It was almost as if she was trying to get back at me for something.

She also reported that, after the birth, the farmer asked a little girl to name the calf. I guess the girl wasn't clear about the route the calf had taken, though.

Welcome to the world, Stinky-Poo-Poo-Head. I hope your next appearance isn't in a bun.

It's Not a Pet Store—
It's a Zoo

One day I ventured into the newest type of mega-store. I've gotten used to buying my groceries in a store the size of Rhode Island. I've come to accept that if I want a package of nails I should pack a lunch, or at least a sizable snack, before venturing into one of those hardware stores-on-steroids. You can walk for several miles and still not find what you went in there for. At least I can.

The new kid on the big-box retail block I discovered was a pet store the size of a car dealership—and a big one at that. I never realized there were so many different kinds of dog food, or that they came in bags that would feed my dog, Nipper, for at least a year.

An entire wall was dedicated to aquariums. Fish of every color and dimension swam in row upon row of glass tanks. It reminded me of a restaurant I once visited in the Philippines. The place was filled with aquariums and you went through until you found the fish you wanted cooked for your dinner. None of the fish in this pet store looked as if they'd make much of a meal, but their price tags were pretty similar. I'd gladly pay $20 for a good seafood meal, especially if I knew it had just been plucked from the water. I'm not quite so likely to spend $20 on something that will swim around in a tank in my living room for a few weeks, then get laid to rest with a flush of the toilet.

When my sons were quite young, we were given a small aquarium and a collection of goldfish. My oldest, Mike, was about three at the time. He and a friend decided to give the fish a bit of excitement and a change of scenery. They thought the fish might like to go for a ride in Mike's Tonka fire truck. He learned a valuable lesson that day. Goldfish don't make very good firemen. My wife, Diane, ended up holding a funeral mass for the dearly departed fire crew. I don't think our dog at the time was too impressed to see what he considered his big white porcelain water dish being used to dispose of the goldfish remains.

The giant pet store also offered a variety of more unusual pets. Various species of lizards occupied one section. Why someone would want to keep a lizard is beyond me. They aren't likely to fetch your slippers or newspaper. Not that Nipper, the dumbest dog ever to get lost on a single flight of stairs, is likely to do that, either, but at least I won't have to worry about her growing up to look like Godzilla.

They even had a section for frogs. Frogs aren't pets. Frogs are bait. When I see a frog with a price tag of $39.95, I think of the hundreds of frogs my sister and I sold for ten cents apiece to our neighbor when we were kids. Those frogs weren't destined to sit in a glass tank for the rest of their lives. For that matter, the rest of their lives only lasted until the neighbor could get them onto a hook.

There were aquariums containing tarantulas. Now there's a pet. If I brought one of those home, I wouldn't be able to make it run and fetch, but I could probably make Diane run and faint. She shouts a really interesting word whenever she sees a spider. I have absolutely no idea how to spell it, but whenever I hear it, I know there's bound to be a spider somewhere.

I'm not even going to talk about the snakes. Snakes do for me almost as much as spiders do for my wife. I'm always hearing about snakes getting loose in apartment buildings and slithering up a neighbor's toilet. Whenever I visit someone in an apartment building, I always flush the toilet several times to make sure I'm not interrupted by a python when I'm in such a vulnerable position.

I spent nearly an hour wandering around the aisles of the colossal store, taking in the huge array of potential pets, grooming products and pet clothes, not to mention a selection of tapes and CDs to keep your parakeet, canary or parrot amused. After I left, I stood in the parking lot, realizing I had forgotten why I had stopped at the store in the first place.

I know it wasn't for the snakes.

Anyone Know Where I Can Get Some Swans A-Swimming?

Those who have a spare US$13,500 kicking around at Christmas might consider re-enacting the Twelve Days of Christmas. Of course, that price depends on the quality of the gold in the five rings, and the amount of time you want the drummers to drum, the lords to leap, the maids to milk, the pipers to pipe and the ladies to dance. There would, however, be an added expense if the ladies in question were exotic dancers. In addition, the price doesn't take into account overtime, vacation pay or medical benefits that you might have to pay. Some locals of the AMAM/ULD (Allied Maids A-Milking/United Ladies Dancing) also call for child-care benefits in their contracts.

Christmas is usually a housekeeping disaster in our house. I can just imagine the mess all those cows, swans, geese, French hens, calling birds, turtledoves and one partridge could make in our living room. It's bound to be almost as bad as the destruction two teenage boys wreak every other day of the year, although it might not smell as bad as the hockey gear.

Twelve drummers drumming sounds like a migraine in waiting. Just the thought of it brings on one of those flashbacks for me. Those of you who can recall the sixties might remember the proliferation of something known as "the drum solo." Every concert had to set aside what seemed like an hour or two for the drummer to go wild without the distraction of other instruments, singers or a measurable IQ.

I've never quite understood the thought process that went into selecting those twelve gifts, or the apparent appreciation on the part of the recipient. Clearly the "true love" who went on this wild shopping spree a few hundred years ago was either too easily convinced by some medieval version of the Gift Suggestion Bureau or was a sadistic lunatic.

Anyone in their right mind would have to wonder about the mental fitness of someone who would think up a gift like twelve drummers drumming. Not even Stephen King could come up with a villain that demented. He had to be some sort of psycho whose sole purpose in life was to drive the person getting these gifts totally mad.

When the drummers were added to the already large crowd consisting of eight maids, nine ladies, ten lords and eleven pipers, the poor recipient of the gifts had an enormous crowd to feed. That's fifty people if you sing the song with the assumption he only sent each of the gifts once. I've always imagined that on the second day, when the person got the two turtle doves, another partridge in a pear tree arrived. By the end of the song, she had the makings of a fairly nice pear orchard, along with a dozen partridges, twenty-two turtledoves, thirty French hens, thirty-six calling birds, forty-two geese and forty-two swans. Using that method of calculation, I figure the demented true love sent more than 140 milking, dancing, leaping, piping, drumming and potentially hungry people. And what if any of them happened to bring along their spouses and children? Hopefully the recipient lived in a large house.

Luckily swans aren't an endangered species. The twenty-three (or, potentially, 190) birds, and the eight (or forty) cows would be enough to supply a fairly nice barbecue, but man doesn't live by turtledove alone. Odds are that no one thought to bring along a salad or plate of Christmas cookies. The poor recipient probably had to pawn the only half-decent gift she got, the five (or, if she was lucky, forty) gold rings to get vegetables, desserts and enough stuffing mix to fill all those bird carcasses.

If I had been one of those drummers, pipers or lords, I think I would have been a little concerned about the mental state of the person singing the song. Surely, somewhere around the fifth shipment of calling birds, she had a nervous breakdown. That can be the only explanation for her continued reference to the gift-giver as her true love.

I'll admit my poor wife has to put up with a lot living with someone like me. At least she'll never have to clean up a mess like the one the Twelve Days of Christmas gifts would leave behind. It would be too cruel to put her through the stress of having all those people, birds and cows invade our home, and expect her to tidy up afterward.

I'd hire a couple of the maids.

Absolutely No Broccoli
Was Injured During the
Publication of This Book

It Might Be Good for What Ails Ya

*E*veryone has been told, at one time or another, to eat a disgusting vegetable or take a gag-inducing medicine because "it's good for you." My mother provided us with a well-stocked cupboard of concoctions that were purportedly "good for what ails ya." Several more botanical mysteries could be found on our plates for the same reason.

It would appear that too many people have listened to their mothers instead of their taste buds. This is further proof that too much broccoli can, indeed, cause a severe reduction in both the brain cells and the will to live.

There are always people whose taste buds are so compromised they can eat just about anything without understanding how bad it tastes. These people don't cause anyone except their children grief about what should and shouldn't be put in the mouth. Their common ancestor was probably the first person who said, "Sure, but can I put some garlic butter on that before I eat it?" when someone dared him to eat a snail.

It's not the well-meaning, granola-for-brains, let's-all-eat-a-hibiscus-on-broiled-tofu crowd we have to watch out for. These are just vegetarians. They're reasonably easy to get along with, good with animals and housebroken. We carnivores look at them as mildly eccentric and harmless. Besides, it means more triple cheeseburgers with bacon for the rest of us.

Then there are the vegans, a much stauncher, provisional wing of the lips-that-touch-spareribs-shall-not-touch-mine set. Vegans don't merely abstain from meat. They break into a sweat at the thought of eating eggs and milk products, because, "well, you know, like, they were once inside an animal, eh?" Unlike quiet vegetarians, they can get more vocal than a rookie nonsmoker about the benefits of a newfound way of life. For some reason, their opposition to eating animals, or their by-products, doesn't seem to prevent them from wearing leather shoes.

Beyond the Planet of the Vegans, it only gets sillier. Hardly a month goes by without somebody resurrecting an ancient healing practice to use against today's viruses. Admittedly some of them are used routinely by other cultures. They have been imported to North America by recent immigrants. Many of them go against the taboos of our culture, just as many of ours are taboo to them.

The mere thought of eating or drinking these medicinal delights makes me think of *Macbeth*'s three witches. These tasty treats don't involve filling up cauldrons with eye of newt and wing of bat to make haggis stuffing. Bear gallbladder and rhino horn on a bed of linguini seems to be more in favor now.

As far as I'm concerned, if people want to eat a bear's gallbladder, they should go into the woods and negotiate a trade with the bear. Perhaps offer it their own gallbladders in return and, just to be polite, offer to let the bear take theirs out first.

A symposium on another, albeit wildlife-friendly, remedy was reported in the press a while ago. Leading the list of proponents for this 5,000-year-old therapy were actress Sarah Miles and the late Indian president Morarji Desai, who died at the age of 99.

In a 1944 book, a British author claimed he had cured himself of tuberculosis, and subsequently treated others successfully for gangrene, cancer, leukemia and heart disease using this practice. The key ingredient is plentiful and is said to contain hormones, enzymes, vitamins and minerals that can even cure AIDS.

These cures are bunk, according to mainstream physicians. (For his sake, my mainstream physician had better think so.) However, you can almost be certain this therapy will cure your mother-in-law's hypochondria. It could also be used as a tool to cure drug, alcohol and tobacco addictions. If, after each cigarette, shot or fix, an addict had to follow this regime, addiction-treatment programs would turn out abstainers faster than ever thought possible, and with virtually no recidivism.

It would also be much more effective than soap in your children's mouths, especially when they repeat the language you've used when you're talking to the idiot ahead of you in traffic who sits mindlessly reading the paper through an entire advanced-left-turn signal.

The symposium was held in Panjim, India, and was attended by nearly six hundred delegates from seventeen countries. The reports didn't mention Canada, but we can be pretty sure some healthier-than-thou bureaucrat from Wealth and Helfare Canada latched onto this cure-all for his boondoggle of the month.

The recommended treatment regimen, for those who wonder if it can cure the pain of psoriasis, male-pattern balding or coughs caused by colds, is to follow a strict diet, abstaining from alcohol, meat, tobacco, tea and coffee. (So far so good.) In addition, though, you have to drink one or more glasses of your own urine every day. As well, you have to have your body massaged, using stale urine that's at least four days old.

It's enough to make tofu sound appetizing.

I'm Not a Cajun Ant, but I Could Be an Ostrich

Somehow it could only have happened in North Carolina. That's the state that thrives on people in North America putting things into their bodies that really shouldn't go there.

The state's economy runs largely on the production of tobacco products. It's also one of those states that makes you think *Forrest Gump* was a documentary. They still believe Andy of Mayberry fame was one of those reality-based cop shows. Now they'd like it if y'all would hunker down for a nice snack of Cajun ants and mealworm spread, and go ahead, have yourself another cigarette while y'all are at it. Take two. They're small.

The people responsible for Bugfest '96 in Raleigh, North Carolina, pointed out that insects are a major ingredient in the foods of a great many cultures. These are the kind of people who believe that, just because something is done in another culture, it has to be good for you. They neglect to note that the average life span in these societies is somewhere around forty-five years, and that insects are one of the leading causes of death—right up there with malnutrition and military dictators.

We've become so focused on health and longevity that we're willing to try just about anything offered to us as long as we're told it's healthy, natural, organic or range-fed. Let's not forget diet, low-cholesterol, fat-free and, that bane of human existence, high-fiber.

A few years ago we got hooked on fiber when granola became a necessary part of every North American's diet. No one ever bothered to ask, "Why am I eating something that looks and tastes like hamster food?" We just followed along because it was supposed to clean out our colons.

Most of us didn't even know we had a colon, let alone that it was clogged with the remnants of every steak we had ever eaten. I'm told that approximately ten per cent of our body weight is sitting around doing nothing in our colons. I'd probably feel a lot worse about the stuff in my colon if I wasn't able to tell myself with absolute certainty that not one milligram of it came from eating Cajun ants and meal-worm spread.

That doesn't mean I'm adverse to trying something new. A while ago, much to the horror of my son, Brad, I ate ostrich. Ostrich farms have become big business in British Columbia. The first time I saw one I thought I had stumbled onto the set of the *The X-Files* when the bird emerged from the early-morning mist. I had never seen ostrich meat on a restaurant menu before, and when I did, I ordered it just to see what all the hype was about. Brad was particularly upset because apparently "ostriches are cool." Actually the piece I ate was quite hot, served on a bun with tomato and lettuce and, surprisingly, didn't taste like chicken.

Over the years, I've dined on everything from barbe-cued bear to beaver burgers. I've eaten fondued moose and reindeer steak. I was even served rat once, but not told what it was until after I ate it. I won't do that again. I've also eaten, and quite enjoyed, barbecued rattlesnake. Surprisingly it does taste a lot like chicken.

In the Philippines, I was given something called *balut*, which looked like an ordinary boiled egg until I opened it to find myself face-to-face with the baby duck that had called the egg home. I would have passed on that, but I was under the Filipino equivalent of a triple-dog dare, and therefore had no other choice but to close my eyes and pray the critter wouldn't fly back up. The people in the Philippines think these mouthwatering morsels are an aphrodisiac. Believe me, sex was the farthest thing from my mind after eating it. Determining the shortest distance to the great white porcelain baby-duck depository was pretty much the only thing on my mind. Some prayers just don't get answered.

There are certain things humans aren't meant to eat. Ants and mealworms must be near the top of that list, right up there with broccoli and Brussels sprouts and baby ducks. Rest assured, I'll never eat anything that was once a bug or a rodent or a part thereof.

I've got to run. I'm barbecuing hot dogs for dinner.

Welcome to Earth,
Turd Rock from the Sun

Over the years, I've been called a good "it." On the other hand, I've also been told I'm full of "it." Now I discover I might be here because of "it." In fact, so might all of us, as well as the birds and the bees, the flowers and the trees and, of course, broccoli. I could believe the part about broccoli, because I've always thought it tastes like "it."

Scientists have traced our ancestry back through Neolithic Man and all the other lithics to various gorillas and apes. That theory has been pretty well accepted now, especially by anyone who has ever wandered, unprepared, into a biker bar. But what came before we were the planet of the apes? What happened before the first fish decided to quit the school and go for a stroll along the beach? What about even farther back to a point in time that my sons might even believe was before the birth of their mother and me?

Scientists have never come to a solid conclusion about how the chemicals needed for life managed to develop on early Earth at a time when the conditions here were just a little hostile. Andrei Arkhipov, of the Institute of Radio

Astronomy in Kharkov, Ukraine, thinks he has the answer. In a controversial article published in *The Observatory*, a well-respected astronomical research journal, Arkhipov wrote that life began on Earth just after the planet cooled down and ran into extraterrestrial "it" that was floating in space.

Obviously the editors of *The Observatory* thought Arkhipov's theory was pretty good "it" or they wouldn't have printed the article. But a lot of other people are saying it's nothing but a load of "it."

Basically his theory states that long ago, in a galaxy far, far away, a planet developed the technology to explore space. These early astronauts, much like ours today, had to deal with doing in space what gets taken for granted on the home planet. When Mother Nature, although she may have gone by some other name, like Gzryklax Mptsfluzx, called, certain bodily functions had to be dealt with. Again, like today's astronauts, these other star trekkers didn't want to have bits of sewage floating around the spacecraft, so they tossed it overboard. "It" was left floating in space, along with the results of many other calls from Gzryklax Mptsfluzx.

One day a small, insignificant planet floating around the universe ran smack dab into a whole mess of "it." Inside the alien "it" were the freeze-dried bacteria, viruses and microbes that eventually became you and me, the birds and the bees, the flowers and the trees and a thing called broccoli.

Even religious groups are joining the discussion about Arkhipov's theory. Nicholas Coote, a representative from the Catholic Bishops' Conference in Britain, says the idea isn't that far removed from the biblical account that God created us from dust.

"It isn't a very inspiring idea," said Coote, "but it would be funny if it were true—and I presume God must have a fairly vigorous sense of humor."

The Reverend Clive Calver, on the other hand, is

obviously one of those people who think Arkhipov is full of "it." He called the theory "speculative in the extreme." Then he went on to say, "First we read that we are the creation of God, then scientists say we are descended from apes. Now they say we're some sort of alien poo. How much further can we sink?"

Boy, I bet he's going to get into trouble when word gets out he uses language like that. I didn't think reverends were supposed to say words like *poo*.

As with all theories, this one brings forward many questions:

- What could the extraterrestrial astronauts have possibly eaten that eventually led to the creation of the giraffe or the duck-billed platypus?
- Does this explain why so many things "taste a lot like chicken?"
- Did Saddam Hussein originate from some sort of undigested bit of bad meat?
- Did alien fast food produce the cheetah, Donovan Bailey and Michael Jordan?
- Was it something's right wing that ended up as Newt Gingrich or Rush Limbaugh?

If this theory is true, it puts a lot of new responsibilities on the shoulders of the people behind the US space program. If we are the by-product of a jettisoned in-flight washroom holding tank, we could be passing on the source of life to some other unsuspecting planets that will eventually come to the same conclusion Andrei Arkhipov did. The NASA kitchens should be very careful what they send along for in-flight meals.

After all, do we want to get the blame for another planet's broccoli crop?

Sure, I Eat Lots of Vegetables

Over the years, I've made my position on vegetable consumption pretty clear. I'm convinced that, aside from various insects, bacteria and viruses, Pandora's box also contained broccoli, cauliflower, turnip and many other disgusting botanical life-forms.

This public stance has, however, created a false impression that I don't eat vegetables at all. Nothing could be farther from the truth. While I would probably be somewhat miserable if I were forced to live a vegetarian lifestyle, and I'd likely be suicidal if I had to become a vegan and give up meat *and* cheese, I wouldn't starve. In fact, most of my daily nutritional intake is comprised of vegetables.

Diane regularly comments about how few vegetables I will actually eat without complaint. I have a simple rule about what I will and won't eat. If it smells like a gorilla's armpit, I won't put it in my mouth. If vegetables are looked at simplistically, this pretty well limits me to peas, corn and carrots. Broccoli, turnip and most other cooked vegetables fall under that gorilla's-armpit rule.

Everything on the planet is animal, vegetable or mineral. I avoid eating rocks at all times, so my diet is comprised of products that fall into the other two categories. Despite ruling out many vegetables from my diet, I still contend I eat a large variety of the ones that don't smell or taste like something that shouldn't be put near your mouth. I'm just a bit more creative in my quest for good-tasting vegetables. I don't limit my flora to the disgusting lumps of matter thrown on a dinner plate beside the meat.

One of my favorite vegetables is wheat. This is a very adaptable vegetable. While I don't think I'd enjoy a handful of raw wheat, I do like it cooked, especially in a cake, a doughnut or a pie crust. Since bread is basically cooked wheat, a ham sandwich is a good source of vegetables. Taking that a step farther, a cheeseburger in a wheat bun, with tomato, pickles and onions, contains more vegetable matter than meat. McDonald's should think about adding that to their next advertising campaign.

Wheat is in another of my favorite vegetable-based meals. The average pizza has a little bit of meat tossed on it here and there, plus a healthy amount of cheese, but the crust, most of the sauce and several of the other key toppings are all vegetables.

I regularly combine some of my favorite vegetables with meat, or something that passes for meat. For example, how appetizing would a hot dog be if you didn't surround it with a cornucopia of vegetables. Mustard, green relish, ketchup, onions and, of course, a wheat bun turn the plain old wiener into a vegetable-rich meal. Make it a chili dog and there are more vegetables than meat.

If you stop by a bar on the way home from work, you're just finding another, more interesting way of consuming your vegetables. Beer is practically vegetable soup with barley, hops, malt and other grains. Whiskey is just liquefied grain. Wine is simply grape juice with an attitude. These fermented vegetable juices can, of course, lead to addiction and a variety of other health problems, adding weight to my argument that vegetables can be dangerous if not consumed in moderation.

Many people forget that the dessert menu is, to a large

degree, a fancy way of disguising vegetables. If you've been brought up to believe vegetables must be served only with the main course, you're missing an entirely delightful way of getting your daily intake of plant products. Remember, chocolate is a vegetable, too. Therefore a hot fudge sundae with a maraschino cherry and chopped nuts is loaded with vegetables. If you're really stuck on the idea that vegetables should be served hot, have a cup of coffee or tea with your dessert.

The snack-food aisle at the grocery store should be moved to the produce section. Potato chips, popcorn and virtually every other item along the aisle are vegetables disguised to look appetizing. Along the same vein, if you need a quick vegetable fix, look no farther than the candy counter. Chocolate bars, mints, nuts and even licorice are all vegetables that are a much tastier alternative to parsnips. Even sugar is a vegetable. Therefore, what better way could you find to eat your vegetables than a package of chocolate-covered almonds?

Correctly claiming you eat a lot of vegetables comes down to counting your entire daily intake of botanical matter. Regrettably I don't expect Diane or my doctor to see it that way.

A Waist Is a Terrible Thing to Mind

When I was a kid, people said I was "big for my age." Now that I'm in my forties, I'm still big for my age. Like many people, I've often used the excuse that I'm just big-boned. Yes, my bones are probably bigger than average, but they haven't changed in size since I was sixteen years old. What hangs from those bones, however, has gone up by about fifty per cent since then.

Over the years, I've lost weight several times. In total I've probably shed the equivalent of the combined tonnage of the offensive line for the Green Bay Packers. The problem is that I've put the same amount back, with a small field-goal kicker added for good measure. I've tried quick diets, long, slow diets, health clubs, self-help groups, herbal products, diet shakes, low-calorie programs and diet pills. I've even resorted to drinking a gallon of water every day. The only reason that works, though, is because you spend so much time in the john you don't have time to eat.

Still, I'm determined to take off pounds. I've been doing research and have discovered startling facts that contradict many of the ideas I had about food, calories and weight loss. Some readers might have jumped to the same confusions, so I'll share my newfound knowledge.

It is possible for round food to contain calories. I had always thought calories needed corners to get stuck in. It turns out, though, that foods like pies, tarts, doughnuts and cookies can actually be loaded with calories. Brown foods like chocolate bars, pecan pies and honey-glazed doughnuts have just as many, and in some cases more, calories than green foods like celery, cucumbers and lettuce. Slicing something doesn't necessarily let all the calories escape into the atmosphere. All these years I thought pizza was the perfect diet food because it was round and sliced. Any wayward calories that might have gotten wedged against a piece of pepperoni or a mushroom would escape as soon as the pizza got sliced. You can imagine my surprise to learn that pizza still contains calories no matter what shape it comes in and how much it's been sliced. Even more surprising was my discovery that frozen foods like ice cream have calories. I learned in high school science that a calorie was a unit for measuring the amount of energy needed to heat something. From that day on, I've been convinced that, since there isn't much heat in a triple-scoop banana split, there couldn't possibly be many calories, either.

As you can well imagine, I'm feeling somewhat deflated now that all my theories about calories have been defeated. Unfortunately no matter how deflated I feel, it hasn't had much impact on my waistline, which is as fully inflated as ever. I'm struggling to resist the urge to turn to some pleasurable activity like getting good and stinking drunk to regain my spirits. Apparently all the really fun spirits like gin, vodka and Scotch are also loaded with calories.

It's only natural to deflect the blame for our failures in life onto some other person. If I really wanted to blame someone else for my weight problems, I'd have to say it's all my wife's fault. Oh, sure, lots of husbands can blame their wives' cooking for a few extra pounds here or there. But I'm talking about a much greater increase in my human proportions than that. I finally realized why it's all Diane's fault. Since my weight didn't become such a challenge until our children were born, I can only assume I've never been able to lose the weight Diane gained during pregnancy.

I don't need a diet. I need a Cesarean section.

Whoever Said Getting There
Is Half the Fun
Never Had to Fly with Me

Surviving Flying Babies

Flying from Canada's West Coast to Ontario is no big deal for the average traveler. For those of us who live under the curse of the evil goddess of airline flight attendants, however, flying is a difficult and unpleasant task.

Some people might think it's silly that I believe I'm living under a curse designed to make all air travel disagreeable. I have undeniable proof, though. A Boeing 767 aircraft holds more than two hundred passengers in relative comfort, but somehow I always get the seat beside the Baby from the Poopy Lagoon.

If there are 205 passengers, 204 of them will be adults. Passenger 205, however, will be under the age of two, hyperactive and largely ignored by passenger 204, who carried him or her onto the aircraft. Passenger 203, aka me, will be expected to sit quietly while the child "entertains" himself or herself.

Oh, the fun a baby can have sitting for five hours on an airplane. There are so many new things to do, exciting things to see and strangers to annoy. Mommy will sit right there, blissfully watching the in-flight movie, occasionally napping and completely oblivious to the aroma wafting from the child's butt. I, on the other hand, can't concentrate on the movie, thanks to the dear, sweet, cuddly, little cherub beside me who keeps ripping the headphones off my ears. Those wires make such great playthings.

Two hours into the trip the flight attendants start serving the in-flight meal. Airline meals have never been known for their palatability but, unless you've traveled next to the Baby from the Poopy Lagoon, you can't begin to understand how unappetizing an overcooked sausage can look. The child's diaper must be an industrial-strength model because, based on the smell, it now holds about half the child's body weight. Mommy, of course, still hasn't noticed because she's enjoying the movie and the child seems to be having such a good time entertaining the man at the end of the row.

If the mother notices the child at all, she's probably thinking how wonderful it is to have a child who travels so well. Isn't it cute how Mommy's Snooky-Wooky is expressing his artistic talents by finger-painting the man's jacket? she's saying to herself. He's so creative. How many other children would think to use that man's scrambled eggs as an art medium?

Looking back on the days when my own sons were that age, I remember how impressionable they were. According to child psychologists, it's a time when children quickly learn new concepts, physical abilities and words.

On a recent flight, when once again I was sitting beside a bundle of joy, I had the opportunity to test this theory out. The child's mother was ignoring a prime opportunity to teach her child new words, so I thought it might make the time go faster if I helped the little dickens with his language development.

Smiling at the mother, who couldn't hear a word I was saying because of her headphones, I whispered to the infant, "Santa bring drum set."

The child gave me one of those cherubic grins that might have been cute if his face hadn't been covered in my breakfast and he didn't smell like the Baby from the Poopy Lagoon.

"Saba ding dumset," he announced.

After a few tries, the child was merrily repeating a fairly understandable version of "Santa bring drum set." The mother just smiled. I figured she was happy to have the egg-covered man entertaining her little darling. I quickly learned not to encourage the child to clap his hands when he spoke. I was afraid it might distract the mother's concentration on the movie, and it seemed to increase the intensity of the baby's diaper aroma.

Buoyed by my first success, I continued educating the child. "Mommy's packing extra pounds," I said.

"Mommy estra powds," he parroted, obviously getting into the spirit of the game.

When we had mastered the commentary on Mommy's weight-control problem, we moved on. By the end of the flight, the child had a vastly improved vocabulary.

The mother was in an obvious hurry to make a connection with another flight, so she was one of the first to deplane. Despite all the hustle and bustle, I could hear the child shouting, "Mommy's not a natural blond!"

I wonder where he learned a thing like that.

Freeway Flashes

I'm everything from the mailboy to the CEO around this multihundred-dollar corporation known as my home-based business. I work in a luxurious office decorated with dinosaur wallpaper, a remnant from a time when this was a child's bedroom.

I had no difficulty getting used to the easier commute to and from work. Usually the only highway problem I face is when I get myself stuck in traffic on the information cul-de-sac. Thankfully I have an in-house computer consultant in the form of my son, Mike, who can act like the traffic reporter on the radio, guiding me out of whatever has tied up my Internet driver.

Even so, I have alternate routes for my commute to my office, two doors down the hall from my bedroom. If traffic backs up near the off ramp to the main bathroom, I take the longer, more scenic route through the kitchen, dining room and living room. If I take this route, I can even stop along the way for a coffee and a bagel. I usually take the bathroom route away from the office because it lets me avoid the late-afternoon construction delays in the kitchen, where my teenage sons are demolishing the grocery budget.

Unfortunately, one morning, I had to relive the horrors of my old commute downtown. Diane, who I've been married to for more than a quarter century, needed a ride to her office because her car was in the shop being fixed. The drive wasn't pleasant.

Lately Diane has been experiencing a few—make that quite a few—of those you-ain't-a-spring-chicken-anymore hot flashes. She insisted the air-conditioning be on full blast. While she sweltered in the cool morning air, I started to feel icicles forming in my nether regions. The chill in the air got a lot frostier whenever I tried to adjust the thermostat. The last time I saw that look on her face she was in labor doing a fairly good impersonation of Linda Blair in a scene from *The Exorcist*.

Aside from the dangers of dealing with the Wrath of Diane whenever I casually tried to sneak the thermostat up a few hundred degrees (on the Kelvin scale), I was faced with the single most dangerous live hazard on our roads today—*commutus obnoxiousi*, more commonly known as Other Drivers.

I've had three run-ins with members of this species in the past. As a result, I now drive a two-wheel-drive, four-on-the-floor wheelchair with leather upholstery. That morning they were out in droves—entire herds of wild-eyed, sleep-deprived, caffeine-deficient, confused, bothered and bewildered Other Drivers.

That day's experiences with these savage beasts was partially my own fault. I was dumb enough to venture into their habitat at 6:30 in the morning, one of the times when Other Drivers are known to be at their worst. The only time that sightings of crazed Other Drivers is higher than during the morning rush hour is at the peak of the afternoon rush hour.

The male of the species is sometimes called the Wet-Lapped Swerver because he tries to steer, hold a coffee, answer the cellular phone and insert a stress-reduction cassette tape into the stereo. The female Other Driver is also called the Ruby-Lipped Twit. It does all the same things as the male, plus puts on makeup while driving.

I, and I'm sure everyone else, have several other names for them, but they can't be repeated in polite company. My personal list of epithets for them is long and colorful and is the reason why my family won't let me get a public-address system installed in my van.

It's probably just as well I don't have an onboard PA system. There would probably be a *commutus obnoxiousi* stampede if we had broadcast what Diane said to me the last time I tried to adjust the van thermostat.

Flights of Antsy

They were offering free sight-seeing flights at British Columbia's Pitt Meadows International Airport and Chinese Restaurant the other day. My son, Mike, gave the best rendition of teenage wistfulness he could while begging to go for a flight. He finally clinched the deal by offering not to point out the number of new gray hairs he could see sprouting on my head.

Actually he reminded me a lot of myself when I was younger. I used to employ that wistful look while hanging around an old grass runway, hoping some pilot would take pity on me. It often worked, and I would look at my house and school from a thousand feet up. Usually these flights were in old, wooden-framed, cloth-covered planes that had been built twenty years earlier as training aircraft in the Second World War.

Since that time I've learned something very important about flying.

I hate it.

If we were meant to fly, we would have come equipped with airsick bags.

Several years ago I was on a plane that lost the automatic pilot somewhere over Northern Ontario. The rest of the flight felt as if we were on a roller coaster. The flight attendants explained that the crew had to fly the plane by themselves and that they couldn't keep the plane as level as the automatic pilot. I would have thought they had to pass a course called Keeping the Plane Level.

No one ever said how the automatic pilot got lost, but my theory was that he was sucked into the stratosphere after flushing one of the onboard toilets. Flushing airplane toilets creates a huge suction that has been known to grab and hold unwary passengers who subscribe to the flush-while-still-sitting method.

I stand as far away from the thing as possible and try not to look into the vortex it creates. It has an eerie resemblance to the special effects in science fiction movies. Getting too close to that vortex could land you on the planet Zargon. Perhaps that's where the automatic pilot is today.

Onboard toilets aren't just a danger to the passengers and crew. There was a report recently about a couple who were sitting in their living room when an alien spacecraft crashed through their ceiling and onto the floor between them. At least they thought it was an alien spacecraft. As the blue-green shimmering craft began to warm up, they came to the unmistakable conclusion that the entire contents of an airliner's waste-holding tank had been sucked through the vortex and had landed as a frozen boulder in their midst. They didn't say if they found an automatic pilot inside the aromatic lump.

Moments after takeoff on my very first flight in a large airliner, the loud thud of the landing gear retracting into its compartment startled one of the passengers.

"Did you hear that?" he demanded. "An engine must have fallen off. We're all going to die!"

It was quite upsetting for the other passengers, who all looked as if they were considering the possibility he might be right. Luckily the flight attendants are trained in how to deal with situations like this, and it wasn't long before they had me calmed down.

Before boarding our free flight, Mike and I had to attend a preflight briefing. The instructor said things like "This is the chronoaltimeter disinflagerator. Whatever you do, don't touch it."

After about twenty minutes of identifying things found in the cockpit that neither one of us understood or could pronounce, we headed for the plane, promising we wouldn't touch anything.

The pilot assured me that the four-seat airplane didn't have any vortex-generating toilets or automatic pilots who got up and wandered around until they got lost. When we were airborne, though, he did the unimaginable.

He turned the controls over to Mike.

I don't mean he let Mike hold the steering controls while he did the actual flying. He let go of everything, and there was Mike, touching all those things we had promised not to touch as the plane made a sweeping circle. Thankfully the pilot took over for the actual landing, but wouldn't you know it. The pilot turned the controls back over to Mike so he could play chicken with the other planes on the runway.

After we stopped and they had pried my fingers off the grab bar beside the window, Mike announced he would need an increase in his allowance to cover the $5,000 cost of getting a pilot's license.

It's enough to make me want to jump onto the next ice cube through the vortex for the planet Zargon. I bet the landing gear doesn't go thud there.

Driving Miss Demeanor

Because of my track record when it comes to people ignoring the strategic location of my rear bumper, I have to be a bit warier on the road. The more I drive, the more I think I should take up a safer method of transportation.

Hang gliding would probably be safer than the roads I have to drive on. There are several groups of crazies driving out there. What follows is a select few.

The Exercise Nut

This is the driver who will stop traffic ahead of you and do a twenty-minute workout. The exercise regimen finally ends when he has his car parallel-parked. In the meantime, he'll go in and out of the parking space countless times, trying to fit a Honda Civic into the tiny gap left vacant by a convoy of Mack trucks.

The Supermodel

This driver always has to look her absolute best. In the event that some flaw might have been created in her mascara because she had to stop at a red light, she'll spend the entire time checking and reapplying her makeup. If she hasn't finished the Tammy Faye Bakker look when the light turns green, she might start to drive while continuing to look in her mirror. More than likely, she'll just sit there. Her appearance is vitally more important than the schedules of the fifty drivers lined up behind her. If she chooses the former, some fool always decides to let her know the light has changed by honking at her. She'll give the inconsiderate peasant the one-finger salute and continue with her makeover.

The Speedophobic

No, this isn't a driver who's afraid of trying to fit his beer belly into a teeny-tiny bathing suit. This driver stakes his claim on the fast lane by cruising along at twenty miles per hour below the posted limit. After all, the sign only refers to the maximum speed. There is nothing mentioned about a minimum. He is often found on the mountain roads of British Columbia, panic-stricken at the wheel of his motor home because "Back home in Alberta we ain't got no hills like these."

The Speedophile

Again, this isn't a driver who cruises around looking for people in tiny bathing suits. Even if he wanted to, he would only get a short glimpse because he only has two speeds: fifty or more miles per hour over the posted limit and stop-at-the-beer-store.

The Audiophile

I'm very familiar with this driver. An audiophile was the first driver to rear-end me. The accident left me permanently disabled. The other driver had been looking for a cassette tape on the floor of his car that, admittedly, was more important than knowing I was stopped ahead. This is also the driver who motors past your house at one o'clock in the morning with his car stereo on full volume and full base. He wants to be certain you have a clear understanding of his "musical" tastes.

The Bumper Buddy

These drivers keep as close to your rear bumper as possible. They are saving money on fuel by using you as their personal airfoil. They need to save all they can in order to pay for their elevated insurance premiums because they've rear-ended so many drivers. Some of them get so close that when they push in their cigarette lighters you feel a warm glow.

The Mobile Office

It's too much to ask some drivers to keep their attention on the road. These people are clearly busier, and therefore more important, than every other driver. Your personal safety is meaningless compared with the deal they're trying to make. You can often see them holding a cellular phone with their shoulder, a cup of coffee in one hand and a pen in the other. All the while, they're reading their notes or other documents instead of watching the road ahead. It gets even hairier when they try to read the tiny print on the stock-market page.

Aside from these, there are those who are just plain bad drivers. Recently it was discovered that several thousand drivers tested at the Richmond, British Columbia, licensing center were only asked one question and not required to take the road test. The question was: "Do you have $550?" The driving examiner in question pocketed the money and the people left with their driver's licenses.

To those of you who may have recognized some of your driving habits here, I have a small piece of advice. Take the freaking bus!

Pure Animal Lust
in the Back of a Pickup

It's about time something was done about people driving pickup trucks when they'd be better suited to a Ford Tempo, and the effect this can have on the increasing population of unwanted puppies.

I live in a rural area outside Vancouver, British Columbia, that's becoming urbanized faster than a developer can say, "Hey, look at that piece of land with all those disgusting trees, birds and animals. It would look much better if it had 150 identical condominiums covering it."

That statement begets the arrival of bulldozers, which beget the houses that bring with them a plague of noxious real estate sales-locusts. The real estate sales-locusts leave behind 150 citified, white-wine-spritzer-drinking junior accountants and corporate-executive wannabees. Now that they have their eleven-hundred-square-foot, three-bedroom, one-and-a-half-bath country manor on a 0.005-acre estate, they all have one thought in mind: "Gotta get me a big fancy pickup truck with four-wheel drive, a cellular phone, and a laptop computer mounted between the seats."

The truck will never be used for any of the functions it was designed to carry out, like hauling manure, bales of hay or fence posts. Instead it will spend its useful life commuting between its owner's condo and the office twenty-five miles away in downtown Vancouver. Its huge engine won't be needed to transport heavy loads or to pull a horse trailer. It will sit idling in rush-hour traffic, adding several tons of hydrocarbons and gases to the smog in the Vancouver area which, on a bad day, can rival Los Angeles's. The cellular phone and laptop computer will give its owner something to do when he gets bored with mundane activities like paying attention to what's going on around him on the road.

There will come a day when he'll look into the box of his pickup truck and realize there's something he should be carrying back there to help him fit in with the rest of the urban pickup cowboys. He'll get the biggest dog he can find, not thinking of the responsibilities that ownership of such an animal brings with it. Since he perceives himself to be a "real man," his dog will have to be equally capable. His "real dog" will never darken the door of a spay-and-neuter clinic.

Two of these individuals were in front of me in traffic the other day as we waited for a tugboat to pass through a swing bridge. In the boxes of their spotlessly clean pickups were the obligatory dogs. The German shepherd in one carried on a lengthy conversation with the Labrador retriever in the other amid much tail wagging and pacing.

As traffic started to move, the dogs tried to continue their conversation at an increased volume until the next traffic light. Clearly they had gotten to know each other pretty well by this point, and it would appear there had been a certain amount of negotiation going on in their conversation. When both vehicles came to a stop, the German shepherd suddenly leaped into the other truck. What took place then, despite the snarled traffic all around, was an enthusiastic session of raw, down-and-dirty animal passion and unprotected sex.

The driver who now carried the two canine lovers must have been oblivious to the whole event, because when the light turned green, he started to drive off. The now dogless driver obviously hadn't noticed the activity, either, until he saw two sexually active dogs pass his side window as they tried valiantly to maintain their balance and complete the job at hand, or rather, paw.

He must have said to himself, "Gee, that looks like my dog doing the humpty dance with that Labrador," because he looked at the dogs, then quickly into the back of his truck.

The other driver continued merrily on his way until he noticed the dogless driver wildly honking his horn and leaning out the window, shouting, "Hey, my dog! Stop!" When he checked his rearview mirror, all he could see was his dog doing the wild thing with a German shepherd. He hit his brakes, causing a rather sudden, climactic moment in the canine carousing amid much disgruntled yelping.

As I passed the scene, the two owners were arguing about whose fault the little tryst had been. By the sound of it, each was trying to blame the other guy's dog.

As for the dogs, who were once again on their feet wagging their tails and discussing the arrangements for visitation rights, I hoped they enjoyed it as much as all the other drivers who witnessed the event clearly did.

What If Flight Attendants Said What They Really Mean?

ecently I did one of those things I really don't enjoy. I placed my life in the hands of a group of people who no doubt spent the better part of the previous night sitting in a hotel bar. They put me into a cramped, uncomfortable position and strapped me down. My wheelchair and crutches were taken away and hidden somewhere, leaving me no way to run, not that I'm much good at running anymore, anyway.

I don't fly much these days, either, but in the years BC (before collision) I spent a lot of time in airliners. I was well on my way to membership in the million-mile club when I was injured. Somewhere around the hundred thousandth mile I stopped enjoying the experience.

The thing that bothers me most about flying occurs before the plane finishes taxiing to the runway. I realize it's the law, but I would be just as happy if the flight attendants didn't tell me how to prepare for my imminent death in the event of a mid-flight incident. Of course, they don't put it that way, but everyone onboard knows what they're really saying.

"In the event the pilot forgot to check the fuel gauges

before we left the terminal, or if the maintenance people went on their coffee break without tightening the engine bolts, we'd like to lull you into a false sense of security about your chances of survival.

"Should we be over water when we run out of fuel, your seat cushion turns into a handy flotation device. You'll also find a self-inflating life jacket under the seat. If you manage to survive the impact with the ocean surface, you won't have time to use the jacket before the plane sinks. Even if you're able to pull the cushion off your seat, get out of the aircraft and inflate the life jacket, you'll be a shark snack before anyone comes to rescue you.

"If the engines fall off while we're over land, you'll be instructed to return your seat to the upright position, close your tray table and put your head between your knees. That way you won't see your pilot and the rest of the crew putting on their parachutes. While in that position you might consider coming to terms with your maker through quiet prayer. You'll also find it much easier to kiss your butt goodbye with your head down there.

"Decelerating from somewhere around six hundred miles per hour at thirty thousand feet to approximately zero miles per hour at an altitude of zero feet is almost always fatal, but it's not a sure thing. Occasionally there are a few survivors. To increase your chances from one in a few hundred trillion to one in a few hundred billion, we recommend you remove any sharp objects from your pockets. Wouldn't it be annoying to survive the sudden impact with the earth, the flaming ball of aviation fuel and the suitcases falling from the overhead compartments only to be killed by a cheap ballpoint pen through your heart?

"From time to time, airliners experience a sudden depressurization. This is usually caused by a terrorist's bomb opening a big hole in the cabin, the pilot pushing the wrong button because he's too hung over from last night at the airport hotel or all the onboard toilets being flushed at the same time. You'd be surprised to know how often it happens because of midair collisions with alien spacecraft.

"If this occurs, oxygen masks are supposed to drop from the console above you. There is a chance you won't have been ripped from your seat and ejected out the gaping hole in the airplane. You may even survive having all the air sucked from your lungs. If you determine that you're still alive and the system opening the mask compartments actually works, place the mask over your face and breathe as normally as any of the other panic-stricken, hysterical passengers. If you're traveling with an elderly person, put your own mask on before helping him or her. By holding the mask out of reach for a few minutes, you'll be able to negotiate a better share in your companion's will. Of course, it won't really do you much good, because the pilot will have been sucked out the front window or blown to bits by the bomb.

"Thank you for flying with Upfront Air. We might not get you there, but at least we're honest about it.

I May Have the Right Stuff, After All

Space—the final frontier. I want to boldly go where no other humorist has gone before. Let the force be with me.

When I was in Houston, I paid a visit to the Johnson Space Center, NASA's earthly home. After touring the astronaut-training facilities, I was sure the powers that be would see the value I could offer them, so I volunteered to be the first humorist in space. I was confident I could show everyone I had the right stuff. The people at NASA didn't seem quite so convinced, however.

My first test was on the shuttle landing simulator. I took control of the ship after it descended to eleven thousand feet on a smooth heading for its Florida runway. I tried my best to keep *Columbia* on course, but it wasn't that easy. The shuttle is about as aerodynamic as a concrete block. Whenever I moved the control stick, the spacecraft pitched wildly from side to side and I sent its nose up and down faster than the roller coasters at the Six Flags Over Texas Theme Park. Apparently I'm the first pilot to guide the simulator through a complete loop-the-loop.

As I approached the runway, I managed to level out

and make a perfect approach, if you judge perfection in the same manner as certain budget airlines. I only missed the runway by a hundred feet, but I taxied into an alligator-infested swamp. My instructor said my flying technique was "interesting," but that NASA preferred to bring its crews back to Earth intact. He eliminated "pilot" from my list of potential space careers.

I didn't have much better luck with the navigator's test. Again, it isn't easy to guide a space shuttle from its orbit two hundred miles above the Earth to an itsy-bitsy runway in Florida. For one thing, they didn't provide me with a single map or set of landmarks to work with. Luckily I remembered the route. Unfortunately the people at NASA have some silly rule about keeping the shuttle in the air the whole way. Personally I thought my idea of landing on Interstate 95 near the Florida–Georgia border and driving the rest of the way made much more sense. That way, if we got lost, we could stop at a tourist information center and get directions. Since my instructor failed to see the logic in my thinking, he struck "navigator" off my career-opportunities list.

Next, I tried out for payload specialist. These are the people who get to launch satellites from the cargo bay of the shuttle with the Canadarm. Since it was made in Canada, and I was, too, I figured I wouldn't have any trouble operating it. I was almost right.

I managed to connect the arm to the satellite I was supposed to put into orbit, but the two simulated astronauts who were outside to help messed up my perfect launch. They kept getting in the way whenever I changed my mind about the direction I wanted the satellite to go. If they kept that up, they would jettison any hope I had of landing a payload-specialist assignment. I remembered that NASA wanted to find people who could quickly make life-or-death decisions, so I made a couple. I squashed one of the astronauts between the satellite and the cargo-bay door. When the other one wasn't looking, I swung the Canadarm like a Louisville Slugger and sent him into an orbit that would return him to Earth sometime around the twenty-fourth century.

My instructor didn't quite agree with my method of getting the satellite launched. Apparently I was supposed to use the other two astronauts to help me get it into orbit. Because I wasn't using the Canadarm properly, it only seemed as if they were in my way, when I was actually putting the satellite in their way. Sure, sure, it was all my fault.

By the end of the tests, my score indicated I had killed a total of seventeen of my fellow astronauts, broken the Canadarm, destroyed a $400 million satellite, lost one shuttle in a swamp, gotten another one stuck under an overpass on Interstate 95 and jammed the cargo-bay doors with squashed astronaut parts. Along the way I had died six times.

I assumed my results left me with little chance of securing employment in the astronaut program, but I was wrong. My instructor told me that as soon as NASA needed a middle-aged, overweight Canadian in a wheelchair who wears trifocal glasses, he'd be sure to give me a call.

My bags are packed and I'm waiting by the phone.

Let's Not Have Any Unscheduled, Catastrophic Flight Abbreviations

*J*ust when I thought it was safe to go back in the air . . .

Perhaps if you're reading these words on an airplane, you might want to save this piece to read when—and if—you reach your destination. If you do make it there alive, you won't want to have spent the entire flight worrying about the things I'm going to discuss. If you do become the victim of an unscheduled, catastrophic flight abbreviation, more commonly known as a crash, you won't want to have spent the last hours of your life thinking about air-travel hazards, either.

Over the years, I've had more than my share of experiences and misadventures involving airplanes, airport personnel and other passengers. I had hoped I'd exhausted my supply of bad flying karma but, wouldn't you know it, my in-flight luck just keeps rolling along.

I've never been a fan of takeoffs or landings. Most unscheduled, catastrophic flight abbreviations occur during takeoffs and landings. If there's going to be a pilot error, it's going to happen in the first or last scheduled moments of a flight. The rest of the time the flight crew supervises the automatic pilot, who never makes any of the mistakes that can lead to unscheduled, catastrophic flight abbreviations.

I started off my most recent flight on the wrong foot. I thought I had a direct flight from Vancouver to San Diego. The ticket agent told me I wouldn't be changing planes anywhere en route. She failed to mention that twenty-three minutes after surviving the takeoff, I'd have to start worrying about surviving a landing in Seattle.

I shouldn't be so hard on pilots. In reality, the other passengers can make you far more miserable than worrying about how much bourbon the pilot consumed at the bar in the airport hotel the previous night.

If you sit beside a window, you're trapped. You sit there, hoping your sphincter has the strength to sustain you through the entire flight. The last thing you want to try to do is climb over the people between you and the aisle while worrying about escaping stomach gases and bladder control.

The middle seat isn't much better. Odds are the person on your right will be left-handed, while the passenger on your left will be right-handed. That way you spend the entire meal dodging elbows, and the rest of the flight worrying about the window-seat occupant's sphincter strength, hoping he or she won't ask to get past you to the aisle. If he or she does, you can add worries about his or her stomach gases and bladder control, too.

Sitting in an aisle seat is more dangerous than most daredevil stunts. It's the easiest way to sustain multiple concussions, abrasions and shoulder separations. A mid-flight stopover gives the disembarking passengers the opportunity to slam their carry-on luggage into the side of your head and/or shoulder a second time on their way off.

On the return flight from San Diego, I encountered a new hazard. I had spent the weekend at the National Society of Newspaper Columnists convention, so I was justifiably exhausted by the time I got on the airplane. Thankfully I managed to survive the beating from the other boarding passengers' carry-on luggage, and it wasn't long before I was happily dozing.

My slumber was suddenly interrupted, though, by the urge to ask the flight attendant to roll down a few windows and let in some fresh air. My first thought was that the occupant of the window seat had misjudged the strength of his sphincter, or that he had underestimated the potential escape of his stomach gases. Luckily I was wrong on both counts, but the truth wasn't much better. The woman across the aisle had opened her seat table and was using it as a platform to change the foulest disposable diaper I've ever encountered.

It was an unscheduled, catastrophic flight abomination.

I Hope the Future's
As Much Fun As My Pasture

Take Back the Clowns

I came face-to-face with the personification of my strongest childhood fear the other day. It brought back memories of horrific dreams and a general unwillingness to use the washroom at our summer cottage.

In my world, the bogeyman didn't go bump in the night. Save those fears for other kids and O.J. Simpson's houseguests. My bogeyman went "Ahooogha! Ahooogha! Honk! Honk! Honk!" Other kids imagined that the bogeyman had a skeletal face or blood dripping from a nasty overbite. They were mummies, or zombies, or even the old man down the road. My bogeyman had a huge red nose, rainbow hair and nearly as much face makeup as Tammy Faye Bakker. The monster in my closet was a clown. His evil twin, or perhaps it was Bozo the Clone, maintained a small housekeeping unit under my bed. To make matters worse, they had turned my entire family into their henchmen.

My older brother and sister used every opportunity to put me in close contact with clowns. In the mid-fifties there was a popular television show called *Big Top Circus*. Each week my siblings would tell me that cartoons were about to start. Close to the television, I would sit through a commercial, waiting for Mickey Mouse or Donald Duck to begin. I was too young to suspect anything, even though it was the only time my siblings ever allowed me to have the best spot in the room. As soon as the kid finished yelling, "I want my Maypo!" the face of the biggest, most hideous, kid-scaring, bogeyman in clown clothing would fill the screen. I'd run from the room with tears, or some other bodily fluid, streaming down my legs. (I prefer to think they were tears, and I'd ask that you humor me.)

One could understand such cruel treatment from siblings. After all, there's no greater joy for an older brother and sister than to successfully scare the you-know-what out of the little kid who's taking up too much of Mom's time. But my parents had fallen under the spell of the evil clown bogeyman, as well.

My mother was one of those get-in-get-it-done-get-out people when it came to doing the necessary in the little building out behind the cottage. She could never imagine people who looked upon the "necessarium," as she called it, as a reading room. Actually she had a number of euphemisms for the place. "The room where Lizzie Borden hid her ax" was always particularly chilling. In her later years, she just referred to it as the "euphemism" rather than think up new nicknames for the place.

She believed I should be properly trained in her beliefs. To best accomplish this, she had my father frame a huge picture of a clown's face. It hung at eye level directly across from the seat of honor.

I always marveled at the bravery shown by my father and brother. They were clearly immune to the evil gaze of the clown. Perhaps it was because they had, as I had imagined, fallen victim to the supernatural powers of the clown in the closet, leaving me as the only one to fight his evil plot. For whatever reason, each could spend long periods of time face-to-face with the image of the bogeyman. Maybe they were getting instructions from it on how to terrorize me further.

When my parents passed away, the job of emptying the house fell to my brother. He shipped several boxes of family memorabilia to me. Strategically placed at the top of one of the boxes was the picture of the clown. When I returned from a hurried trip to the euphemism, I picked up the frame and found there was glass on both sides. Turning it over, I discovered the real truth behind the strength of my father and brother. On the back was an equally large picture. Instead of a clown, Marilyn Monroe, clad in nothing but a bit of makeup and stiletto heels, stared longingly through the glass.

Recently I walked into the local outlet of that famous family restaurant chain. As I walked toward the counter, its trademark employee stepped through a door. We nearly collided and stood there face-to-face. The clowns that had haunted my childhood flooded through my mind, although the one in front of me did smell better than the one in the euphemism. All those years of clownaphobia evaporated, and I laughed to myself about it. The clown in my face apologized, and it was as though he were apologizing for all the clowns who had been both visible and invisible in my childhood. I felt so much better as he walked away.

I felt even better when I tripped him.

Curious Cures
for What Ails Ya

I've never been a big fan of home remedies. I was exposed to too many of them by my mother. She was forever trying to feed me something that was supposedly "good for what ails ya," even if you didn't think there was anything particularly "ailin' ya" at the time.

During the last many years of her life, she took to drinking. No, she didn't have a bottle of Scotch hidden in the back cupboard. I think it might have been preferable if she had developed a taste for something alcoholic. When I say she took to drinking, I mean she started drinking an array of concoctions she had read were, say it with me now, people, "good for what ails ya."

One of her favorites was hot cider vinegar with honey. I don't care if it could cure cancer. There was no way I could even get a cup of that near enough to my lips to give it a try. She even substituted plain old everyday hot water for coffee. This is the woman who had, for many years, made a cup of coffee so strong it left you needing sleep again three or four months later. The sudden switch from coffee that I'm convinced she made from nuclear reactor waste water to boiled tap water was supposed to improve her health.

She was only sixty-five when she died.

I think it was the cider vinegar or a severe caffeine deficiency that did it.

My distrust of unconventional medicine was further heightened recently when I paid my monthly visit to my doctor. Amazingly the topic of my weight crept into the conversation. Of course, I've tried virtually every weight-loss method known to man. I can eat watercress and gain weight. I can sit beside someone eating a doughnut and gain weight. The only things I haven't tried are the unconventional weight-loss methods that become popular from time to time, so I thought I'd ask about acupuncture.

"I've had a few patients try it," my doctor said, "but none of them had any success."

I knew it had to be too good to be true. I pictured myself being punctured like a balloon, flying around the room a few times and landing a much thinner shadow of my former self.

"There was an Oriental medicine place in town a few years ago that had a lot of success with a product they were importing," he said, momentarily buoying my hopes. "People were shedding weight like crazy, but after a while they all started to get quite ill. It turned out the medicine place was selling tapeworm eggs."

I told him I'd pass. I wasn't quite that desperate . . . yet.

Despite my reservations about trying to cure myself of anything, I still find myself scurrying to the over-the-counter medicine section of the drugstore every June. You see, I suffer from hay fever. I'm not just allergic to the occasional bit of plant pollen; I'm allergic to the entire month.

I'll do anything short of drinking cider vinegar to get relief from these allergies. I've tried every brand of antihistamine available. I spray in nasal sprays. I drop in eyedrops by the gallon. I'm probably singularly responsible for the defoliation of a few acres of rain forest to supply my facial-tissue needs.

Only another hay-fever sufferer can understand the desperate need I have to relieve these symptoms. My eyes burn. My sinuses ache. My nose runs. I provide entertainment for my caring family when I try to speak.

"Plebe pabs the beanut bubber," I'll say.

I know they can understand me, but they always look at me as if I'm speaking in tongues, grin and ask me to repeat what I said.

"The beanut bubber. I bwanna but beanut bubber on my toas'"

"You want to put peanut butter on your toes?" they ask with glee.

I usually give up and eat my toast dry. There's only so much ridicule a hay-fever sufferer can take from the non-suffering members of his family.

At least I'm not alone. Brad, my youngest son, suffers along with me. His hay fever has long provided him with an excuse for avoiding lawn-mowing duty. Just the thought of cutting the grass can make his eyes water.

Not so long ago, Brad took it upon himself do a bit of unconventional medical research. He made a remarkable discovery that should perhaps be published in the world's leading medical journals. While we were visiting friends, he proved that teenage hay-fever sufferers can indeed mow someone else's lawn.

Especially if the host owns a ride-on lawnmower.

One Size Fits None

I will readily admit that my height and weight are above average. Okay, my weight is even a bit more above average than my height. The last time I fitted on one of those charts that says what you should weigh based on your height was when my father turned to my mother and said, "What do you mean, you're pregnant?"

I'm not an S person. I can't even remember being an M or an L. It's been a couple of decades since I could comfortably call myself an XL. These days I'm either a double or a triple XL. I realize that might sound like some sort of pornographic movie-rating system, but I assure you I'm just talking about my shirt size.

People my size don't venture into typical men's wear stores. We're doomed to search out places with names like Mr. Humongous, Tall Fat Man's Emporium or Big Bubba's Tents and Tailors. *Search* is the operative word in that statement. Stores that stock my sizes aren't very common. It takes me nearly two hours to drive to the haberdashery where I buy my clothes. The law of supply and demand is played out to its fullest in these shops. There isn't much supply, so they demand twice the price for everything.

At least I can be thankful I take the smaller sizes available in these stores. I'm amazed at the size of some of the clothes these places stock. When you get up to 8XL, there's more material in a T-shirt than there is in a queen-size bed comforter. An 8XL leather jacket could put an entire animal species into extinction.

Where I really run into trouble is when someone designates an article of clothing as "one size fits all." I come across this all too frequently in the form of one particular piece of apparel—hospital gowns. What "all" do hospital gowns fit? Pygmies? People with names like Sleepy, Doc and Grumpy? Even if I was a foot shorter and took another foot from my girth, I'd still be concerned about how much of me didn't fit under the swatch of cloth.

I've never been given a "one size fits all" hospital gown with enough material even to begin to cover my "partial," let alone my "all."

Who came up with the idea to call them gowns? I'm six foot four. I have longer shirts. They aren't gowns. They aren't even miniskirts. If I went out into the street wearing a hospital gown, I'd expect to be arrested for indecent exposure. I'd even be willing to make a citizen's arrest of myself if I exposed that much Kirkland to an unwitting public.

Yet what do hospitals do? They make sure you have ample opportunity to display whatever part of your anatomy that doesn't conform to "one size fits all." If you're having an x-ray taken, they make you change into the gown at one end of a hall and then parade you to the opposite end, where you sit with a group of equally attired, or rather unattired, souls. To make matters worse, the hospital staff seem to enjoy making everyone go through this ritual.

"Go to the end of this hall, turn right, walk all the way

to the end of that hall and you'll find the change rooms," they say. "Remove all your clothes and put on this gown and then come back here and sit on one of those chairs until your name is called in an hour or two."

"But I just hurt my finger—"

"The longer you delay, the longer you'll have to sit here."

While you wait your turn, you have to find a way to sit that will serve two purposes. Naturally you need to make sure as much of your "all" is covered by the flimsy material. It's almost equally important to make sure you have gown material between you and the chair. Trying to do both at the same time is next to impossible. Allowing exposed skin, especially the sensitive patch that doesn't normally see the light of day, to come into direct contact with a vinyl waiting room seat cover is just asking for emergency skin-graft surgery. The result is a roomful of people squirming like a bucketful of red wrigglers.

The clothes a man wears can say a lot about his stature. A hospital gown can eliminate all doubt.

I Never Realized Tennis Elbow Could Be Such a Pain in the Butt

I guess the subconscious me must be having a better time than the wide-awake me.

I haven't picked up a tennis racket in thirty years, but somehow I've developed tennis elbow. My doctor confirmed it when I went to see him the other day. The only logical explanation is that I'm playing tennis in my sleep, and enough of it to cause my elbow to hurt when I'm awake.

The only other possibility is that tennis elbow is contagious. My youngest son has recently taken up the sport at school. Perhaps he's a tennis-elbow carrier and transmitted it when he sneezed in the car recently. However I got it, I can assure you I don't want it. Now I have to walk around with a big blue strap around my elbow and do an exercise that sounds so ridiculous you wouldn't believe it if I told you what it was. Suffice to say, it involves canned peas.

I think doctors make up these exercises to see if their patients are really as gullible as they think they are. Just to be on the safe side, though, I bought a can of peas on my way home. I hope no one I know sees me doing what my doctor told me to do with them, though. A lot of my friends, and most, if not all, of my family, are already pretty convinced where I rank on the sanity meter.

No matter what I go in for, no visit to the doctor is complete without a discussion of my girth. I know I'm big, but it seems everyone wants to tell me just in case I hadn't noticed. A while ago my wife and I went to a fast-food drive-through and ordered drinks. She asked for a medium and I requested a large.

"Here's your medium," said the girl at the pickup window. A few seconds later she added, "And your large."

I snapped back, "I know I'm large, but you don't have to rub it in. That's why I ordered a diet drink. Couldn't you hand it to me without making a comment? After all, you're no beanpole yourself."

The girl looked at me with a wide-eyed, slack-jawed expression as I drove off in disgust. I suppose my wife was right when she said the girl was only referring to my drink size, but I'm a bit sensitive about my weight, so people should be more specific.

Writing is a fairly sedentary job. Those of us who don't make our living chasing celebrities find getting up from our keyboards to pour another cup of coffee to be the most strenuous exercise we get in a day. Some days I even skip the coffee. As a result, I'm sure you can guess the advice my doctor gave me after he told me I had tennis elbow.

"You need to get more exercise," he said in one of those matter-of-fact tones that says there really isn't any point asking for a second opinion.

Actually I've always been afraid to ask a doctor for a second opinion. He'd probably say, "Okay, I think you're ugly, too."

"How do you feel about swimming?" he asked.

"It's probably the best way I know to stay alive when you're in the water," I said.

Swimming is supposed to be an excellent form of

exercise. I used to do it a lot when I was a kid. Today I'd be willing to swallow a helium canister if I thought it would keep me afloat. The last time I went swimming someone suggested calling Greenpeace to help guide me back out to sea.

How much good did knowing how to swim do for all those poor people on the *Titanic*? For that matter, you have to pity the ones who were on weight-reduction diets onboard that doomed ship. They didn't just drown. They drowned on an empty stomach. Clearly, for those people at least, swimming and dieting were highly overrated activities.

I left my doctor's office promising to get more exercise. I even agreed to use exercise equipment for at least twenty minutes every day. Now that I've invested eighty-nine cents in a can of peas, I guess I'll have to honor that promise.

Just don't ask me to show you what I'm going to do with it.

There's a Pusher on Every Corner for My Addiction

Newspapers are one of those little things in life that give me a lot of pleasure. Okay, so they also give me my income, but that's another story.

In those "I have to do everything" arguments with my wife, I often hear about how much time I spend reading the paper. I'm a firm believer in sharing the workload around the house; after all, fair is fair. She does eighty per cent of the housework and I do eighty per cent of the newspaper reading and television watching. I've been meaning to point out to her that things have started to pile up with that other twenty per cent of the housework she never gets around to doing while I'm doing my other chores, such as sorting and reading the mail (bills in her pile, *Time, Maclean's* and *The Hockey News* in mine).

Perhaps my lust for the news is an addiction. That way I can say it's not really my fault. Addictions never seem to be the fault of addicts. It's always the environment or dysfunctional upbringing that makes people become hooked. The anticigarette lobby tells us that children who smoke probably have parents who smoked, so it's really their parents' fault. Similarly the population-control groups tell us that most people who have children have parents who had children, too.

It scares the heck out of me to think what I'm going to be blamed for when my kids grow up. Some statistician will come up with something like "Children of humorists are more likely to develop strange outlooks on life." These are the same people who say things like "Ninety-four per cent of serial ax murderers ate mashed potatoes as a child, therefore, mashed-potato consumption can lead to serial ax murdering."

So if I'm addicted to reading newspapers it was my father's fault. He had a routine every evening that included watching the news on our old black-and-white television, reading the newspaper and falling asleep until my mother woke him up to tell him to go to sleep. I once thought a great Halloween costume would be to carry a newspaper around in front of my face and say I was disguised as a father. Dad squashed that idea, of course. Not because he was embarrassed by the image of him it would project; it was just that he hadn't read the paper yet.

My addiction to newspapers started out small. I'd sneak the odd peek over Dad's shoulder or read the articles on the back page when he thought I was playing at his feet. Soon I moved up to sneaking off with the whole paper before he got home, and then ironing it with my Tonka steamroller so that he wouldn't become suspicious.

By the time I was fifteen, I had a two-paper-a-day habit. It wasn't long before I started on expensive imported newspapers. I had to hide my growing addiction from my parents, so I'd sneak the papers into my room in my school bag. Burning incense hid the smell of printer's ink.

My parents, of course, started to worry. It was the late sixties, and parents were always on the lookout for drugs. They were never quite sure what to look out for, but I was doing a lot of the things they had read about in the "How to Tell If Your Child Is Taking Drugs" pamphlet that came inside a carton of cigarettes.

"Does your child speak in monosyllables or grunts?" Of course I did. I was a teenager. All teenagers go through the "yep," "nope" and "gmuhg" stage, not just the ones who have smoked a few joints.

"Does his money disappear as soon as he gets it?" It sure did. The *Sunday New York Times* was expensive.

"Is he displaying mood swings?" What teenager doesn't? My most severe mood swings occurred on statutory holidays when the presses didn't run.

Newspaper addiction is more prevalent in men than women, but it's often women who suffer the most when they're married to an addict. I was shaken into getting my addiction a bit more under control the day I saw an ad showing a woman's picture beneath a large-type caption saying: "Harry, this paper is the only thing you pay attention to, so pay attention to this. I've left you!" Even though the name was wrong, I had to go find my wife to make sure it wasn't her picture.

Both of my sons have the early-warning signs of becoming news addicts. The biggest fight of the day between them is now centered on who has first dibs on the paper. The oldest one has been slipping away from home earlier in the mornings and coming home later after school. His mother and I are worried. He might be sneaking into the school library and reading a paper.

When we asked him about it, he said, "Gmuhg."

Needles Make Me Feel
So Unwelcome

Needles don't bother me. I know some people who, at the thought of getting a needle, feel all squoodgy-woodgy. (Squoodgy-woodgy is, I believe, a medical term that, in layman's terms, means "I'm gonna hurl.") If you're one of those people, perhaps you shouldn't read any further.

I was eight when I overcame my fear of needles. It was spring, the time when a young man's fancy turns to climbing through muddy fields to build dams on streams. Together with a like-minded group of my buddies we hiked a mile or so back into the fields.

Of course, spring is also a time when young men develop a hint there might be more to this world than climbing through muddy fields and building dams. The chain of events that started that day would leave us all feeling pretty confident about our manhood.

We found her lying at the edge of a snowdrift near a grove of trees that served as a windbreak for an old, unused lane. Something was clearly wrong with her, and one look made us all pretty keen to help her. She offered no resistance as we wrapped one of our jackets around her unclad body. Despite her mud-caked red hair and the blank stare in her deep brown eyes, we could all see that, given better circumstances, she was clearly quite a fox.

Okay, okay, you can all snap your imaginations back to reality. What we had found was a sick red fox.

Together we carried her to the office of the local vet. We were all expecting a hero's welcome for our act of kindness to this tiny animal. Our names would be in the newspaper. Local citizens would point us out on the street. We would be heroes for other children to emulate.

When the vet opened the bundle, he recoiled in horror. The words that came from his mouth sounded nothing like the praise we had been expecting. Our intelligence was questioned, as was the marital status of our parents. We had brought him a rabid fox. To be perfectly accurate, it was now a rabid former fox, because it had succumbed to its fate somewhere on the trip.

Our parents were summoned, as was the local doctor. The vet explained to them what their little darlings had done. He also pointed out that rabies is a disease of the brain, and since we were all clearly lacking in that area, we might not have to worry. The doctor said that, even though the fox had been too weak to bite any of us, we were still at risk because of the possibility of becoming infected through a cut or scrape. His recommendation: a needle in the stomach every day for two weeks.

Our names did appear in the paper. Mothers would point us out to their children, admonishing them not to do anything as stupid as we had done. Each afternoon, right after school was let out and our friends retreated to the baseball diamond, we eight lined up in the doctor's office while he injected us in assembly-line fashion. By the end of the ordeal, we had all lost any fear of needles. We could all stand tall as our classmates whimpered at the sissy little needles the school nurse gave out every year. We were men. Come to think of it, the school nurse looked a little like she could have been a man, too.

To this day I'm not bothered by needles unless I'm told I'm about to be injected with a radioactive fluid for a bone scan. I've had several of these over the past few years, and I always expect to come out as a mild-mannered writer by day and a crusading night-light in the evening. "Evil darkness is erased by the glowing skin of . . . Humorrrrr-Mannnnn!"

The fear isn't caused by the needle per se. It's more from the recurring thought that if this is such a safe procedure, why is the technician wearing so much lead?

My mind drifted back to those days recently when my doctor ordered a blood test. You see, I need not have any fear of Dracula. Any vampire who would choose me as its evening meal would either have to be on a severe diet or contemplating a suicidal hunger strike. My blood is locked deep inside me and it won't willingly come out.

Knowing this, I gave fair warning to the unsuspecting lab technician who had the unfortunate luck to serve me. She confidently said, "I always get it on the first try." Within minutes she knew the taste of defeat, the same way a pitcher does who watches his no-hitter evaporate as the last opponent in the ninth inning sails a home run over his head.

After several attempts on both arms, she decided, as many more before her had, that trying to extract blood from the inside of my elbow was useless, so she moved on to try the back of my hand. In order to increase her chances, she put my hand under the flow from the hot-water tap. As I stood there with warm water running across my hand, I had the immediate sensation that signaled I'd have no trouble providing a urine sample should one be required.

After inserting the needle and moving it around deep inside my hand, she discovered that once again she had a dry well. The sound of a chain saw at a work site next door gave her an idea, which I quickly vetoed.

Finally she decided to prick the end of my finger. She seemed quite pleased when she warned, "This is the way that hurts the most." For the next five minutes, she worked on my finger as if she were a dairy farmer trying to get milk from an old barren cow. When she finally secured about two milliliters of my blood, she gave up. Between my blood, and her sweat and tears, she had enough to do the test.

As I was leaving, she offered some simple advice should I need a blood test again. It was the same thing the vet had told me in 1962.

"Don't ever come back here."

Not This Week, I Have a Headache

I woke up one morning with a mind-numbing headache. As a result, I spent the better part of the day fretting about what I would write my column about that week. Twelve hours later I was still sitting in front of my computer, trying to think about the column that was due on my editors' desks the next day and wondering if I might be having an aneurysm.

It wasn't just the regular, run-of-the-mill headache. It was one of those types that seem to encircle your whole head—across the forehead, behind the ears and along the back of the neck. When I rubbed my forehead, the back of my neck hurt more. When I rubbed the back of my neck, it felt as if my brain were going to pop out the front of my forehead. Even my eyelids hurt. I think I might have sprained them trying to keep them open while I chauffeured one of my sons that evening. No matter how lousy a parent feels, it can't interfere with a teenager's schedule.

There were a number of things that could have caused this particular headache. I tried to identify them in the unlikely hope I might come up with a way to get rid of it.

Perhaps it was the rather nasty midwinter cold that

had snuck up on me a couple of weeks earlier. Half of the people I talked to were suffering with the same symptoms— a cough, a sore throat and a general feeling of ill will toward the other half of the population who weren't suffering. When you're sick, there's nothing more annoying than talking to someone who's healthy. That's especially true when the healthy someone is your spouse.

Wives have very little sympathy for husbands who are brought to the edge of death's door by a bad case of the sniffles. They don't understand, or perhaps they don't care, that we men are convinced we might not survive without mega-doses of sympathy, tender loving care and maybe a back rub or two. A bowl of chicken soup prepared the way our mothers used to make it might be nice, too.

The headache could also have been caused by a lack of sleep. It had been quite hard to get a good night's sleep when my wife kept waking me up to tell me my cold-induced snoring was keeping her awake. Somehow she had thought that, just because she had to get up at 5:30 a.m. and drive to work in the morning, I should stop waking her up. Didn't she realize I was sick and needed my rest?

It might have been stress that was making me feel like Lizzie Borden had buried her hatchet in my forehead. Most people who meet me think I'm laid-back and relaxed. It's all a charade. Inside, I'm worried sick about a lot of things. For example, at that moment I was under a lot of financial stress because it was getting close to the time of month when we had to go grocery shopping. I think there are Third World countries that get by on budgets smaller than what it costs us to get past the check-out line at the grocery store. That's enough to give anyone a headache.

Perhaps it was allergies. I tried to think if anything new had come into the house that might be causing a reaction. Maybe it was my youngest son's new CD, the one he had been playing over and over since he'd bought it the day before.

Some people say animal companions can do wonders for people who aren't feeling well. Those people have obviously never experienced a headache in the same house as Nipper, the dumbest dog ever to get lost on a single flight of stairs. My dog seems to believe it's her duty to let me know everything that goes on in front of our house. In her loudest bark, she has to announce every child who rides a bicycle along the sidewalk and every cat that strolls through the garden. If I don't go to the window to see what she's barking at, she assumes I've gone deaf and will run around the house until she finds me so she can repeat herself even louder.

Of course, there was always a chance that my headache might have been caused by sitting all day in front of my computer, pounding my head against the keyboard, trying to figure out what I was going to write about that week.

I Miss Horsing Around

I was reminded of one of the things I miss the other day. It's been nearly nine years since my spine was damaged, and in that time I've become more or less used to the limitations this condition has placed on me. There are, however, some things I truly miss.

I miss the feel of hot, sweaty flesh pounding rhythmically beneath me, and the sounds of heavy breathing and snorting as I arc up and down—at times barely able to avoid falling off. I miss the rush it gave me as it forced adrenaline through my system.

It's not that I experienced it very often and, frankly, I wasn't all that good at it, but every time I did it, I had a great time. Had I known that I'd have to stop doing it, I would have done it a lot more when I could. That's why I find it hard to believe there are people out there who have no desire even to try it. I'm sure some of you take doing it for granted. I did. I now wish I hadn't, of course.

Yes, I sure do miss the joys of riding a horse. Well, what did you think I meant?

For several years, before the arrival of our first child, Diane and I lived on a hobby farm in the country, south of Ottawa, Ontario. Many of our neighbors were horse breeders who gave us the opportunity to ride without having to experience the opportunity of cleaning stalls every day.

I loved one particular stallion with an uncomplimentary, although quite fitting, name—Tank. Like all horses, he had an official, more pretentious name, which wasn't used very often. Tank's other name was Manotick Fats, a moniker that combined the town of his birth—Manotick, Ontario— and the size of his girth, which was massive. In a way, I guess we were kindred spirits. He was half-Belgian and half-standardbred. At six foot four, I was one of the few people who could comfortably ride him.

My experience with horses had been limited before my first ride on Tank. My only other ride, bareback with a friend, was on a horse that had become spooked by a swarm of wasps it had annoyed by stepping in their nest.

I quickly realized that sitting in a saddle, atop an unspooked horse, was much more enjoyable. Nevertheless, slowly walking around the edge of a twenty-five-acre field got boring after a while, so I asked Bruce, Tank's owner, how to get the horse to move faster.

"Tank only has two speeds," he said, "slow and stop-to-eat, but you could try standing in the stirrups and yelling."

I was unaware that Bruce was a notorious practical joker.

Building up my courage and mentally determining that all my affairs were in order, I circled the field a couple of more times. Finally, at the far corner of the field, I took a deep breath, stood and emitted a mightily impressive "Yeeeeeee-ha!"

Tank rose like a helicopter and met me coming down as he was lifting off. I instantly knew that my nether regions were going to be a bit sensitive for the next few weeks. We landed several feet from our liftoff, and immediately launched skyward again.

We crossed that field in seconds. I can still close my eyes and picture Bruce waving his arms wildly and diving out of our way as Tank leaped through the gate and into the next field. With each landing, I revised the length of time I expected to be speaking in a voice one or two octaves higher than normal. Finally the sight of some tasty alfalfa growing along the edge of the field got Tank to shift into stop-to-eat.

It was Diane who sustained the most serious injury of the day. Her horse, an aging Arab that had been saved from a career in the adhesive industry, watched what Tank was doing instead of what it was doing and tripped over its own front legs, throwing Diane and separating her shoulder.

People were amazed that, considering my limited equestrian experience, I managed to stay on for the entire ride. I'd like to say it was my incredible balance, profound athletic ability and sheer determination that kept me in the saddle. The truth was, when I stood up, my feet became wedged into the stirrups so tightly that no horse could have ever thrown me.

Tank is long gone, as is my ability to ride. I miss them both. If I had it to do all over again, I'd do it all over again . . . but with a layer of foam rubber between me and the saddle.

Kirkland's Rules to Live By

Reaching the status of a middle-aged North American apparently gives one the power to dispense advice to the rest of the world about how to live life properly. Some people believe the only qualifications necessary for this activity is a kindergarten education and a five-book deal from a major publishing house.

I beg to differ. Life can't be learned from a book. Life must be experienced or, failing that, learned from a newspaper column like mine. Therefore, for those without the time or patience to go out and experience life on their own, I'll pass along a few simple rules to live by, ones that would have saved me a lot of unwanted or unpleasant experiences had I known about them ahead of time.

Five Basic Survival Skills

- Avoid accidentally hitting the car horn when following a procession of motorcycle gang members
- Never open a conversation with "Are you putting on a little weight?"
- Never agree with someone who starts a conversation with "I think I'm putting on weight"
- Never get into a cab bearing the bumper sticker, "I Brake When the Voices Tell Me To"

- Make sure your designated driver understands the words *nonalcoholic beverage*

Five Rules for a Peaceful Marriage (Male)
- Understand that, even if a man is speaking in a forest with no one around to hear him, he'll still be wrong
- Accept that no matter what she says, you'll eventually be saying, "I must have been mistaken"
- Know all her likes and dislikes—there are frequent pop quizzes
- Learn the difference between washable and dry clean only
- Appear interested in the minutest details of her day's events

Five Rules for a Peaceful Marriage (Female)
- Marry a man who understands that even if a man is speaking in a forest with no one around to hear him, he'll still be wrong
- Marry a man who can accept that no matter what you say, he'll eventually be saying, "I must have been mistaken"
- Marry a man who knows all your likes and dislikes—even when you change your mind
- Marry a man who knows the difference between washable and dry clean only
- Marry a man with so little life of his own that he'll be interested in the minutest details of your day's events

Five Rules for Achieving or Maintaining Financial Security
- Don't have children
- Don't have children

- Don't have children
- Don't have children
- Don't have children

Five Rules for Maintaining Your Sanity
- See Five Rules for Achieving or Maintaining Financial Security
- Do not try to program your VCR, microwave, wristwatch or anything else in a package labeled "Easy to Operate"
- Never, ever, buy a computer
- Buy preassembled bicycles
- Never tell a three-year-old anything that could elicit the response, "Why?"

Five Rules for an Enjoyable Meal
- Do not eat broccoli, Brussels sprouts, turnip or anything else that smells like a boiled sneaker
- Do not watch a four-year-old eat
- Do not laugh with a mouthful of hot coffee
- Do not make the people across from you laugh if they have a mouthful of hot coffee
- Don't think about the value of the groceries your teenagers are consuming

Five Rules for Living with a Teenager
- Learn the 3,482 definitions for the phrase, "Yeah, whatever"
- Never insinuate you have a sex life
- Don't listen to the lyrics of whatever it is he or she is listening to
- Understand that anything over two years old is an antique
- Blame yourself for ignoring the Five Rules for Achieving or Maintaining Financial Security

Five Rules for Easy Dealings with Government Officials
- Never call a government information line
- Never cross an international border
- Never ask questions when paying for a government service
- Just do what they say, even if it contradicts common sense
- Speak slowly and never use monosyllables

Five Rules for Home Buyers
- Always look for the high-water line on the basement walls
- If there's no high-water line on the basement walls, check the first- and second-floor walls (believe me, I wish I was making this one up)
- Never believe the statement, "Those tracks are hardly ever used anymore"
- Find out the answer when you hear yourself saying, "I wonder what kind of animal lives in that burrow under the back porch"
- Set aside a little extra money for the usual repairs, and a lot of money for the truly unusual and spectacular ones

One Rule for an Exciting Life
- Ignore the above rules